General editor
Peter
Herriot

New
Essential
Psychology

Individual
Differences

D1166210

Vivian Shackleton Clive Fletcher

Individual Differences
Theories and applications

Methuen

London and New York

First published in 1984 by
Methuen & Co. Ltd
11 New Fetter Lane, London EC4P 4EE

Published in the USA by
Methuen & Co.
in association with Methuen, Inc.
733 Third Avenue, New York, NY 10017

Typeset by Rowland Phototypesetting Ltd
Bury St Edmunds, Suffolk
Printed in Great Britain by
Richard Clay (The Chaucer Press) Ltd
Bungay, Suffolk

British Library
Cataloguing in Publication Data

Shackleton, Vivian
   Individual differences.—(New
   essential psychology)
   1. Individuality
   I. Title   II. Fletcher, Clive
   III. Series
   155.2'2   BF697

ISBN 0-416-33760-0

Library of Congress Cataloging in
Publication Data

Shackleton, V. J.
   Individual differences, theories and
   applications.

   (New essential psychology)
   Bibliography: p.
   Includes indexes.
   1. Individuality.   2. Difference
   (Psychology)
I. Fletcher, Clive.   II. Title.
III. Series.
BF697.S46 1984   155.2 84-9137
ISBN 0-416-33760-0

Contents

1 Introduction

This book is about the psychology of individual differences. It is concerned with the ways in which psychologists have seen people as different from one another in their ways of behaving, thinking and feeling. Since psychologists have, for the most part, seen psychology as a science of behaviour, what you will find within the covers of this book is mostly scientific psychology. That is, there is an emphasis on objectivity, rigour, measurement, testing and experiments. The trouble is that within a scientific psychology of human behaviour, individual differences can easily get lost.

Experimental psychology

One branch of scientific psychology, experimental psychology, has concerned itself much more with general processes such as learning, thinking, memory and perception than with individuals. General theories have been formulated which look at how people (that is people in general) learn, think, remember, and so on. Although the raw material, the subject matter, of the experiments are obviously collections of individual people (or 'subjects', in the terminology of laboratory psychology), the preoccupation has been with the ways in which people are alike, rather than different. And their behaviour is examined in controlled, laboratory conditions.

Taking an example helps highlight the common approach of the experimental psychologist. Let us take the topic of vigilance. This refers to the process by which people are able to select out of a mass of information the occasional key piece they require. A classic case is someone looking at a radar screen on board a ship. Most of the time there will be blips, tiny flashes or 'noise' on the screen which are of no consequence to the radar operator. They represent waves, driftwood, another ship in the convoy or electrical 'noise'. This may go on for hours. The job of the radar operator is to spot the occasional blip which might represent an enemy submarine, ship or plane and which the operator should do something about. The psychologist might be interested in the practical problem of how to improve the chance of the operator successfully spotting and acting on the enemy-ship blip, and not acting on a 'false positive' – the driftwood blip on the radar screen. Typically, the experimental psychologist will bring the task into the laboratory and design experiments to tell him or her how long the typical subject should perform the task before vigilance performance deteriorates significantly, what the lighting levels should be, or how much training is required to reach an acceptable standard. Now these may be important, practical questions for the applied psychologist to ask. They may have an important bearing on theories of attention or perception for the theoretical psychologist. But they are concerned with the general principles of rest pauses, lighting, training or attention based on groups of people. The experimenter pays little attention to the fact that different individuals might react very differently to the experimental situation. The experiments do not tell us much about individual psychology, about the ways in which individuals differ on the task. They are not usually designed to tell us whether men do better or worse than women, experienced operators differ from inexperienced, older people differ from younger, extraverts differ from introverts, and so on. And they certainly are not designed to tell us whether *this* operator is better than that one, and if so, why.

Correlational psychology

There is, though, another branch of scientific psychology which is much more interested in the ways that individuals vary one from another than in general processes or trends. This is individual difference psychology, sometimes called 'differential' or 'correlational' psychology. Before we go into details of this method of investigation, though, we need to say a few words about what a correlation is. A correlation between two sets of scores reflects the degree to which they vary together. It is measured by a correlation coefficient which varies from zero, reflecting no relationship between the two variables, to -1.0 or $+1.0$, meaning perfect negative or positive correlation. A negative correlation signifies that as one factor goes up, say speed of driving on a motorway, another variable goes down, say miles per gallon of petrol. A positive correlation obviously means that the two variables go up or down together (say income earned and amount of money saved, or hours of sunshine at Blackpool and sales of sun-tan lotion).

However, it is very important to beware of the risks of reading too much into a correlation. An association between two factors is not proof that one has caused another. For instance, a study once showed that cigarette-smokers did worse at college than non-smokers. This could be great news for the anti-smoking lobby. It might appear that the way to do well is to give up smoking. Or that smoking dulls the brain. In fact, we cannot say any such thing. Just because course marks and smoking are correlated does not mean that smoking leads to poor marks. The fact that B follows A doesn't prove that A caused B. It might be the other way round. Perhaps poor marks lead people to take up smoking, to relieve the anxiety. But this, too, is just as likely to be false. Much more likely is that both factors are the product of a third factor. Studies have shown that introverts do better at college that extraverts. We also know that introverts are more likely to be non-smokers than are extraverts. So perhaps this accounts for the relationship. The point is that it is easy to fall into the trap of believing that correlation equals causation, when it just isn't necessarily so. Bearing this caution in mind, we can now return to individual difference (correlational) psychology.

The approach of correlational psychology is to single out a trait, say intelligence, and relate this to other variables. The first step is to design measuring instruments to examine how individuals differ on this trait. A particular individual can then be described by a score on the trait. Scores on the measuring instruments (often called 'tests') are then correlated with scores on other instruments or with performance on a range of behaviours in different practical situations. For example, intelligence-test scores might be corre-

lated with scores on a personality questionnaire or with performance in school. This gives us a view of how individuals behave in
different situations based on different trait measurements. But
measurement of traits is more difficult than the manipulations of
variables in an experiment, and we cannot be sure of cause-and-
effect relationships, as we can with laboratory psychology. The
characteristic of a designed experiment is that subjects are treated
with certain manipulations so as to discover relationships between
the 'treatment' and other measurements. So if we wanted to test
the effect of alcohol on driving, we might select certain subjects,
allocate them to two groups, and give the control group no alcohol
and the experimental group four gins. Half an hour later we would
put the subject on a driving simulator and note any differences
between the groups. Assuming there were significant differences
and provided the groups were similar in all important respects
except for the manipulation of alcohol, we would be able to say that
alcohol affects performance on the driving simulator. We would
be able to state cause and effect.

As regards individual differences, though, we cannot usually
conduct our investigations by laboratory methods. This is because
we cannot manipulate a subject's personal characteristics – age,
sex, personality, intelligence, social class, and so on. Subjects
bring their personal characteristics with them to the psychologist,
who can observe and measure but not manipulate. So we use
correlational designs and do not infer cause and effect without
other evidence.

The risk run by those who concentrate on individual differences by the correlational method outlined above is that, again, the
uniqueness of individuals can get lost. First, it is open to the
criticism that an individual is more than the combination of
numerous but separate traits. One current, more recent view is of
human beings as active, aware problem-solvers, interacting with
and construing their psychological world. It is of complex, multi-
faceted individuals, difficult to classify, whose behaviour is dependent very much on the situation in which they find themselves or
which they select for themselves. This is a view we will elaborate in
chapter 5. For the moment we would caution the reader against
over-categorizing an individual into the 'little boxes' represented
by the chapter headings. For clarity and ease of description we
have divided the topic of individual differences into major ways in
which psychologists have gone about describing their fellow
humans. So you will find chapters on motivation, intelligence,

personality, etc. But an individual is very much more than the sum of these components. For example, each of these variables may interact. Thus, an extravert, male old-age pensioner may react to a questionnaire designed to measure his desire to achieve success very differently from an extravert, male 20-year-old student. He may be far less concerned to do 'well' on the test and project an achievement-oriented image of himself. Age alone may not effect the achievement score, but age plus particular personality may. We have tried to make such links between the chapters by referring to topics found in other chapters, but we rely also on the reader to avoid over-compartmentalization.

Secondly, there are undoubtedly certain aspects of individuality which are unique to that individual and which are paid scant regard by correlational psychologists. An oft-quoted comment by Kluckhohn *et al.* (1953, p. 53) is that 'Every man is in certain respects like all other men, like some other men and like no other men.' First, the ways in which he is like all other men include the factors mentioned earlier – the general psychological principles of human learning, communication, human development and similar functioning of body organs. Secondly, the factors he shares with others are the group-related factors such as gender, age and ethnic background. Thirdly, each person's ways of living and behaving have unique elements. These include experience of self, life history and patterns of events that have taken place during development. This book mainly concentrates on the second of these three contributions to individual behaviour, since that is where individual difference psychology has made the biggest strides. It does not ignore the first and third, but assessment psychologists in particular have not focused on the uniqueness of individuals as such, but rather on the ways in which individuals differ. That is on how and how much a particular individual is similar to or differs from other people. Investigating and assessing someone's behaviour 'in the round' needs an awareness of all three – similarities, differences and uniqueness. Each of the three elements converge in the science of the psychology of individual difference.

A third reason why the individual person may be overlooked by correlation psychologists is that correlations between variables in psychology are hardly ever perfect. Physical relationships often produce perfect correlations, say between the mass and weight of a substance. In social science or medicine, correlations are rarely so obliging. The persistence of double-glazing sales people and their sales figures may be correlated and may be based on real cause and effect. But all the persistence in the world may not make Tom a single sale. And while it is now almost certain that smoking is a cause of lung cancer (though only *almost* certain, since the evidence mostly rests on correlations between smoking and cancer), one often hears committed smokers saying something like 'Well, my old uncle smoked 60 a day for 75 years, and lived to be a hundred, so it can't be true.' Correlations are only moderately useful in making predictions in any specific single case. We can say that the probability is that if he smokes heavily he will get lung cancer, but not whether he will or will not. It is a point we will return to in chapter 5 when we discuss nomothetic and idiographic approaches.

Psychologists have not only been concerned to describe and measure individual differences traits. They have been interested, too, in explanations. They have investigated *why* people differ on the traits, on the sources of differences. There are two major threads of explanation. One is that we are as we are because of our genes. The blueprint for our behaviour is laid down at the moment of conception, when the new individual-to-be receives his or her identity from the combination of parental genes. The other type of explanation is that it is our upbringing that determines how we behave. Our experiences and our environment from the moment of conception onwards, not our genes, determine who and what we are. The debate between the proponents of versions of these two views is the nature-nurture debate. Because of its central role in explaining the ways in which individuals differ, it is a major theme running through the book.

Some reasons for studying individual differences

So far, we have pointed out some of the aims and themes of the book – to describe, measure and explain the ways in which individuals differ. A final and important theme remains to be mentioned, the reasons for all this scientific effort. One reason, crudely, is 'because it is there': the need to know. Psychologists have been interested in understanding, in simplifying and ordering the complexity of human similarities and differences, in the relationships between the myriad of different variables used to describe people. As scientists, they look for theories to unify and explain these variables and relationships.

A second reason for investigations of individual differences is to tackle practical problems. These psychologists' researches are motivated more by the desire to answer questions whose answers have an immediate application, than for scientific knowledge *per se*. The questions may be educational (such as to select children for special education), occupational (to recruit people for jobs, for example) or clinical (to identify and help those most in need of special treatment). The results of this work have sometimes been surprising. Over the past fifty years, some of the early and often long-cherished, traditional measures have been exposed as almost worthless. Thus phrenology (head-bump reading), graphology (handwriting analysis) and astrology have been found to be of little or no use. Selection interviews, projective tests and written examinations have been shown to be far less reliable and valid than many would have supposed. One major chapter here, the last, is devoted specifically to the important issue of the application of knowledge, but throughout the book the practical, applied nature of much of the work crops up time after time.

Many may applaud these psychologists' concern for 'real-life' problems. But this concern brings its own problems, the most dramatic being that it has plunged the psychologist into the political maelstrom. Any system which sets out to assess people's characteristics is closely related to socio-political assumptions and influences. The controversy over the implications of different intelligence-test results for blacks and whites in the USA, reviewed in detail in chapter 8, is only the best-known example. Other examples abound. The USSR has officially banned the use of standardized tests (although Brozek, 1972 suggests they are still used), ostensibly because of the hereditary bias of intelligence tests, and group-intelligence tests were discontinued in New York City public schools in 1964. Examination for the purpose of selective education (the eleven-plus), much of it based on intelligence tests, was largely abandoned in Britain by the mid-1970s. Although there is evidence that intelligence-test scores predict later educational achievement, testing and dividing children at 11 years of age on the basis of such scores was not in tune with the prevailing egalitarian and educational philosophy. Science and technology can rarely, if ever, be separated from the socio-political climate. This is especially true of the science and application of knowledge of individual differences.

2 Early work

This is not a history book, and so this chapter will be short. Looking back on early work in the field of individual differences can be interesting and occasionally amusing, but a lot of the time it is also rather unhelpful from the point of view of understanding the present theories. So we will limit ourselves here to a brief consideration of those whose contributions have been fundamental and which one needs to know to appreciate properly the context of more modern developments.

One person in particular is usually identified as the father of the study of individual differences – Sir Francis Galton. In 1869 he published a book, *Hereditary Genius: An Inquiry into its Laws and Consequences*, which reported that in studying the family trees of eminent men, he had observed a strong tendency for eminence (in a variety of fields) to run in families. Galton drew the conclusion from such findings that intellectual ability was determined by heredity. We can now, of course, see a lot wrong with this conclusion. One obvious defect in his work is his inability to explain the dearth of eminent females; since few of them were given the opportunity to reach the heights of achievement (or even to set foot on the lower slopes), it is not surprising that an argument based on the role of heredity comes unstuck here. Although Galton did not completely disregard environmental influences, he drastically underestimated them. Perhaps this is not too hard to understand, given the era in which he lived and the social attitudes and beliefs that were prevalent in the privileged classes. Galton himself was a gifted child (he was able to read before reaching his third birthday) and was related to various eminent people, one of whom had particularly influenced him with his own findings and theory – his half-cousin, Charles Darwin.

Galton's conclusions are not of great interest; his contribution to individual differences lies in the fact that he was perhaps the first person to study them systematically, and with an orginality of thought that led him to formulate many of the key concepts and methods used in the field today. In *Hereditary Genius* he established the principle of looking at varying levels of descent (closeness of genetic relationship) and how they related to measures of ability. He was the first person to advocate the twin-study method of investigating the relative influence of heredity and environment. The general notion behind the approach, much used in present research, is that since identical twins have identical

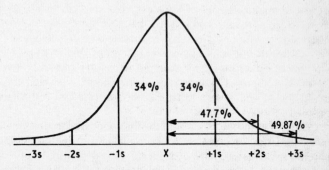

Figure 1 The normal distribution.
X is the mean or arithmetic average; s indicates a standard deviation, a measure of the spread of the data. It is such that 68 per cent of the data fall within 1 standard deviation above and below the mean, and approximately 95 per cent within 2 standard deviations above and below. Thus, we could say that if the mean IQ score is 100, and the standard deviation is 15, then 68 per cent of people will get a score of between 85 and 115. A person getting a score of over 130 would be in the top 5 per cent of the population.

genetic endowments, whereas non-identical twins do not, if we compare them on some quality like intelligence, any greater similarity between identical than between non-identical twins should be attributable to the influences of heredity. This conclusion rests on the assumption that twins of each kind tend to have equal degrees of similarity of environment.

Another of Galton's 'firsts' was to take the mathematical description of the bell-shaped curve we know as the normal distribution and apply it to psychological characteristics (see figure 1). Various physical characteristics, like height, seem to be distributed in this way, and Galton felt that as psychological attributes must have a physical basis, then they should follow the same rules. Irrespective of their relationship to physical processes, it does seem to be the case that many psychological traits and other qualities do roughly follow a normal distribution. Note the word 'roughly'; both natural and psychological phenomena approximate to the normal curve, but a perfect normal distribution is achieved about as often as one comes across other kinds of perfection. The nature of the normal distribution facilitates the provision of descriptive statistics that help interpret, summarize and communicate data. However, since many psychological variables are abstractions (they are not actually 'there' in the sense that weight or colour of eyes are), we can construct our measures of them in such a way as to ensure that they do follow a normal distribution. Modern measures of intelligence are commonly a case of this. But it would be wrong to assume that all traits, etc., have to be so distributed; for example, in chapter 5 we will refer to Eysenck's notion of a dimension of psychoticism, which has a markedly skewed, non-normal distribution (the vast majority of people score very low on it).

Galton was enthusiastic about the idea of mental testing, but he never took this beyond a rather crude level. For the first proper psychological test we have to await the arrival of Alfred Binet. In 1905 he was asked by the Parisian education authorities to devise a method for identifying those children whose lack of success in ordinary schools suggested they needed special education. He adopted a pragmatic approach. Binet, and his collaborator Simon, collected together a large series of short, everyday tasks (such as counting coins) that supposedly sampled the higher mental functions of comprehension, judgement, reasoning and adaptation. These tasks were ordered in terms of difficulty and the tests were administered individually by trained examiners. Binet assigned an age level to each task which was the youngest age at which a child of normal intelligence could complete the task. A child started with the tasks for the youngest age and proceeded up the ladder of task difficulty until he or she could complete no more tasks. A child's 'mental age' was the age associated with the last tasks he or she could successfully perform. Later, other investigators suggested that this mental age could be divided by the true, or chronological, age and multiplied by 100 to get an intelligence quotient:

$$(IQ = \frac{MA}{CA} \times 100)$$

Thus, if a child achieved a mental-age 'score' of 100 months (8⅓ years), and his true age was 90 months (7½ years), his IQ would be

$$(\frac{100}{90} \times 100) = 111$$

There are some strong objections to this notion of mental age. One of them is that Binet seems to have been using a variety of tasks to measure different aspects of intellectual ability at different ages – and so what sense is there in this overall concept of mental age? Nevertheless, full credit should be given to Binet for this first and very worthy attempt to produce a numerical scale of intelligence. He was very modest about it, claiming it was a rough guide for identifying children who needed special educational help, not a true measure at all. He noted that intelligence was too complex to be interpreted and explained by a mere number. Any number gained from attempts at measurement was merely an average of performance on many tasks and should not be seen as a label. These limitations on the interpretation of intelligence have, over the succeeding eighty or so years, often been forgotten by psychologists and others.

In 1916 Lewis Terman of Stanford University published an extensive revision of the Binet test. The Stanford Binet, as it became known, didn't only cover children but extended the measurement up to adult levels. Terman's aim was to make intelligence tests available for the testing of everyone, not just to spot below-average children. His test was widely used for individual testing until just before the Second World War and set the standard for many of the written tests that followed.

Having looked at Galton's methodological ideas and Binet's

intelligence test, the next step in the sequence might be to describe Spearman's work on factor analysis and the theory of intelligence he put forward. But that is rather more contemporary with modern theories and so will be considered when intelligence is discussed in chapter 3. Here, instead, we will turn our attention to some of the early theories of personality.

Beginnings in personality theory

Ideas on personality and how to assess it have a long and varied history (see Welsh, 1982), and for the most part a rather undistinguished one. The first theory of real merit is the one that in the mind of the public is synonymous with psychology, Freud's psychoanalytic theory (see Brown, 1961, for a concise overview of Freud's work).

Freud

Outlining Freud's theory, even very briefly, is no easy task. This is because his theory, or theories, evolved throughout his life, right up to his death in 1939. They were not very precisely formulated or well integrated at the best of times, and the gradual changes in them do nothing to help our understanding. Often his writings permit of a variety of interpretations. However, there are some consistent and clear elements in his thinking. To Freud, personality structure consisted of three interrelated and dynamic systems – the id, ego and superego. The id is the powerhouse of personality, the source of all psychic energy. The instinctual drives of sex and aggression (for that is how Freud saw them) are incorporated in the id, which works on the pleasure principle; it cannot tolerate the tension arising from an unsatisfied drive and seeks to reduce it by immediate gratification of the drive, irrespective of social constraints. The id, though, is unconscious and has no direct access to the external world. To obtain the goal objects that will satisfy drives, it develops an offshoot in the first year of life. This is the ego, and it operates on the reality principle. Basically, its function is to act as an interface between the relentless unsocialized impulses of the id and the reality of the constraints placed on need gratification by society. So, the ego has the job of getting the goal objects that will satisfy the id in a socially acceptable way. It represents the conscious awareness of the world. Alas for the ego, it has also to cope with the third part of the personality system to emerge, the superego. This is like a severe, over-demanding conscience. It is the moral censor of our actions, an internal idealist setting standards for us to work to. The superego arises through the values individuals perceive their parents and society to hold (these perceptions might be quite distorted and unreal) and which they take within themselves. Much of it is unconscious, though some elements are accessible by the use of techniques like free association and are thus, in Freud's terms, preconscious. In its own perfectionistic way, the superego can be as demanding – in the opposite direction – as can the id. Again, it is the ego that has the job of coping and adjusting to the demands of reality.

These three systems are in continual conflict, and compete for a fixed amount of psychic energy. The outcome of this conflict and competition determines much of our behaviour, said Freud. The reader might like to pause and consider whether in his or her case one of the systems seems to have come out on top. Are you a very controlled, realistic, pragmatic type of individual (ego-dominated)? Or are you prone to feeling guilty about things, worried about others' expectations of you, always striving to do better (superego-dominated)? If the id has won the power struggle, you might be impatient, quick-tempered, impulsive and generally rather uncontrolled. Bannister (1966) has humourously and graphically depicted Freud's theory of personality as being like a fight going on in a dark cellar between a sex-crazed monkey and a maiden aunt, the whole affair being refereed by a nervous bank clerk!

There is a great deal more to Freudian theory than these three basic systems in personality. The actual development of personality rests on the individual's progress through a series of psychosexual stages. Libido, or pleasurable sensations associated with body functions, is focused on different zones of the body at various periods in childhood. First is the oral stage (6–12 months), with pleasure being associated with the mouth. Next comes the anal stage (second year of life); with the arrival of toilet training, the anus becomes the centre of attention. The phallic stage follows, when the child is 4 or 5 years old. At this stage, libido is associated with the genitals, and the child experiences strong sexual urges towards the parent of the opposite sex – the famous Oedipus complex. Following the phallic stage, there is a long latency period in which remarkably little seems to happen until the individual reaches the genital stage in adolescence and, if all has gone well in the previous stages, learns to direct sexual impulses appropriately.

The significance of these stages – specifically the first three – is that if the individual experiences problems in going through them, this may leave a permanent effect on his or her personality. The problem can arise through over-gratification of libido (e.g. too much breast-feeding at the oral stage) or through frustration of it (e.g. being weaned too early). Fixation at a psychosexual stage leads to various personality types, according to Freud. Thus, fixation in the early anal stage, when pleasure is associated with expulsion of faeces, leads to the expressive type, marked by cruelty, destructiveness, lack of order and tempestuousness. In the later anal stage, associated with retention of faeces, fixation would result in traits like meanness, obstinacy, precision, and so on (the anal-retentive personality type). There is a fair amount of evidence that many of the personality traits and qualities Freud identified in his personality types do seem to be associated with each other, but no convincing proof that they are related to these early childhood experiences, as he suggests (Fonagy, 1981).

Leaving aside the allegation that the English translation of Freud's works may contain flaws that have misled us, one of the great difficulties with his theory is that it is so vague, and deals with such strong feelings and reactions (many of them unconscious), that it is almost impossible to subject it to adequate experimental test. To be sure, there is no shortage of attempts (see Kline, 1981a), and quite a lot of support is gained for concepts broadly similar to those of Freud, but they are often only *broadly* similar. There is no denying Freud his place as the man who made us think about personality in a radically different way, and his ideas remain very influential; many of the concepts put forward by Cattell, whose theory we will look at in chapter 5, have links with psychoanalytic thought.

Jung

Some of Freud's original disciples parted intellectual company with the Master and went on to develop theories of their own. The ideas of one of these, Carl Jung, have had quite a marked influence on later work in the individual differences field. Jung's theory, known as analytical psychology, is even looser in form than Freud's, and has more of the quality of a philosophy or religion than of a scientific enterprise. The description given here will be limited to aspects of the theory which have greatest relevance for present research.

Jung saw much of personality in terms of a striving for harmony between opposites. The self was the agent for this search for unity, for oneness – a theme which crops up in many later humanistic personality theories (like that of Rogers). In essence, the harmony needed is between conscious and unconscious elements of personality. The unacceptable side of our personality is referred to as the Shadow – the content of which was unconscious and often inconsistent with the social masks we present to the world (in Jung's terms, the Persona). An example of this is our sexual orientation and identity. Jung said that everyone had *both* a masculine, assertive aspect, called the Animus, and a feminine, passive aspect, called the Anima. In males the Animus dominates and the Anima is in the Shadow, while it is the other way round in females. This notion has a strong echo in recent work on sex-role orientation (Bem, 1975).

Much the same principle is applied in relation to what Jung called the 'attitudes' of introversion and extraversion and to the four functions of sensing, intuition, feeling and thinking. The 'attitudes' of introversion and extraversion conform fairly closely to the popular notion of what these words mean, and they are taken up in modern theories like that of Eyesenck and Cattell, though these psychologists refer to them as traits, not attitudes. Whichever attitude dominates the conscious psyche, so the other is correspondingly strong in the unconscious. The same goes for the four functions. These are ways of experiencing the world and dealing with it, and according to Jung one of the consistent differences between people is the priority of functions (which dominate, which are auxiliary and which inferior and unconscious). Again, whatever function dominates the conscious, there will be another that is equally strong in the unconscious. To Jung, overdevelopment or overemphasis of any attitude or function was undesirable, because it leads to neglect of the others. The neglected elements of personality in the unconscious will disrupt behaviour and create tension unless given some degree of expression, rather as a neglected child does something naughty to get attention. A major part of the process of individuation, of gaining self-understanding, is to listen to our unconscious promptings and to integrate them into our normal functioning; as we do this, the conscious part of our personality expands and the unconscious diminishes (Jung, 1928).

Jung's notion of two attitudes and four functions gives rise to a classification of eight main types of personality, of which there is a measure called the Myers-Briggs Type Indicator (Myers, 1980). This particular personality questionnaire has gained in popularity in recent years, as has Jung's theory itself. Is it right to describe people in terms of 'types'? Many psychologists would argue that such classifications greatly over-simplify personality and are to be avoided. Typing people does not tell you how strongly they conform to that type's characteristics, and often they will have important attributes that do not fit the type at all and would thus be neglected if we were to go solely on the type label. The concept of continuity of personality dimensions (i.e. the idea that people range from very low levels of some attribute, like intelligence, to very high levels of it) does not fit very easily into a typological approach. The other point of view, in favour of typologies, would say that it has a valuable function at our inadequate level of knowledge of personality. Proponents of this line of thinking would say, for example, that there may only be a limited range of types of car – saloons, hatchbacks, coupés, etc. – but each particular car has its own attributes in terms of size, colour, engine capacity, and so on. Why should we not think of personality in the same way? As long as there is sufficient similarity between groups of people for a type label to be applied, they would hold, then this is a viable approach.

Having completed our tour of the ancient monuments of individual differences psychology, we will now go on to consider contemporary work, starting in the next chapter with intelligence.

3 Intelligence

'Intelligence', like 'personality', is one of those words commonly used by both psychologists and non-psychologists to describe people. If you ask non-psychologists what they mean by 'intelligence', they will give you words and phrases such as 'common sense', 'nous', 'bright', 'quick on the up-take' or even 'the ability to get on with people'. These convey a socially acceptable cognitive or social skill. A psychologist, when asked the same question, is unlikely to answer so unequivocally. He or she is likely to agree that the term 'intelligence' covers a very varied range of cognitive abilities but that it is impossible to provide any clear indication of what specific behaviours or performances are, or are not, representative of intelligence. Then, they will point out that the definition of intelligence is closely tied to the notion of an intelligence quotient (IQ) score obtained from an intelligence test. Some psychologists go so far as to say that intelligence is what intelligence tests measure since we often define intelligence in terms of the ability to do intelligence tests. Finally, the concept of what intelligence is or means has changed over the past eighty or more years and continues to vary according to the prevailing values of the time, the theoretical view one takes of intelligence and the measuring instrument one uses. All this can serve to confuse or frustrate the student, but it is important to appreciate that the concept of intelligence is not a single scaleable entity like height or weight which can be measured with one simple test. This is one of the ways in which psychology differs from the physical sciences, and it provides psychology with its challenge as well as its frustrations.

The previous chapter provided a brief historical view of intelligence measurement and the aims of those devising tests. This chapter will be concerned with three different theoretical approaches to the concept of intelligence. The first is the factorial approach which relies on test scores, and factor analysis of these scores, to reveal the nature or structure of intelligence. This method could also be called the quantitative or psychometric approach because of its emphasis on paper-and-pencil measurement. The second approach is a qualitative, as opposed to a quantitative, one and is exemplified by the work of Piaget. We will only touch on this approach since it is not really interested in individual differences but is concerned with the progress of intelligence through developmental stages. It emphasizes the increasingly abstract way in which people think and organize their knowledge as they mature to adulthood. The third approach is concerned more with physiological aspects of intelligence and is a newer and rather controversial topic.

Finally, the chapter will be concerned with a completely different theoretical question, the nature–nurture problem. Here we will be interested not so much in the structure or definition of intelligence but in the role of heredity and environment in causing differences between people in measured intelligence.

Theories of intelligence

Factorial theories of intelligence

Before launching into a description of the different factorial theories of intelligence we need first to grasp some of the fundamental ideas behind factor analysis. In fact, factor analysis has had an enormous impact on the whole field of mental testing since the 1930s, not just on intelligence. The description which follows will not go very deeply into this complex area, nor will it go into the mathematics involved. Instead, it will confine itself to examining the logic of factor analysis and to defining some key concepts.

The first concept is a factor. When a number of people answer a series of questions on a test, or a series of tests, some of their answers will be broadly the same. The groupings of these correlated answers represent factors. In other words, factors are the hypothetical entities (neuroticism, verbal intelligence, introversion, etc.) which are measured by tests. Notice, though, that the identification of factors relies on the statistical techniques of calculating correlations described in chapter 1. You will remember that correlation is the extent to which variables vary together. It is measured by the correlation coefficient, which varies from a value of zero (meaning no correlation) to −1.0 or +1.0 (meaning perfect negative or positive correlation). We can build up correlation matrices, which show intercorrelations between tests, and from these matrices look for the presence of factors. Table 1 gives an example, taken from a particularly clear description of factor analysis, published by the Open University (1974).

Suppose that we give four different tests to a sample of people. These tests might be called verbal fluency (VF – say, the speed of generating words about a topic), opposites (Opp. – naming the opposite of a given word), manual speed (MS – say, the speed of tapping a pencil in a certain place) and reaction time (RT – speed of responding to a visual stimulus by pressing a button). We can correlate our sample's results for each of these tests with the results from each of the other tests. Table 1 gives a possible result.

The first thing to notice in this table is that the correlation of a test with itself is high (0.9 for VF, for example), but not perfect. This represents the reliability of the test. Another thing to notice is that one half of the matrix is the same as the other. In other words, the matrix is symmetrical. This is because the correlation of VF with RT is obviously the same as the correlation of RT with VF, i.e. 0.1 in our table. But the main thing to notice is that the matrix

Table 1   Correlation matrix. (After Open University, 1974)

	Verbal fluency (VF)	Opposites (Opp.)	Manual speed (MS)	Reaction time (RT)
VF	0.9	0.6	−0.3	0.1
Opp.	0.6	0.85	−0.1	0.2
MS	−0.3	−0.1	0.9	0.7
RT	0.1	0.2	0.7	0.8

suggests that the four tests are measuring just two factors. The correlation between the two 'verbal' tests is fairly high (0.6) as is the correlation between the two manual tests (0.7), while the correlations between the verbal and manual tests are low. Although we do not know anything about the two factors except that they help us understand the data a bit better, we might call them a 'manual factor' and a 'verbal factor'. So the MS test could be taken as a measure (though an imperfect one) of the hypothetical entity called a 'manual factor'.

Another concept which you often meet in factor analysis is factor loading or saturation. This refers to the degree to which a particular test measures the hypothetical entity or factor. Looking at the table again, we can see that RT and MS load rather higher on the hypothetical manual factor than do VF and Opp. on their verbal factor, and certainly much higher than do the manual tests on the verbal factor. What often happens in psychometrics is that a whole range of tests may have high loadings on a factor such as intelligence, though some will have higher loadings, and so be purer measures of this factor, than will other tests.

So far, then, we have seen that factor analysis tries to reveal structures or relationships that underlie test results. The structure may be simple, showing just one factor, or complex, revealing many factors. At an extreme, there may be as many factors as tests, if each test correlates very poorly or not at all with each of the other tests. Where there are lots of tests, though, the problem of trying to decide how to structure the results becomes much more difficult. There are several methods of factor analysis, each dependent on difficult mathematics, which approach the problem of structuring the results rather differently. So there is a choice of different methods of factor analysis, with some techniques combining the correlations into more factors than others. One method, favoured by Eysenck, concentrates on a small number of powerful factors where the factors are orthogonal (that is independent of each other, where the axes representing pure factors are drawn at right angles). Another method, favoured by Cattell, uses oblique (that is correlated) factors which are often greater in number and so less powerful, but which are designed to make the 'best psychological sense' of the data. In factor analysis, as in other topics of psychology, we find that there is no one clearly defined answer or best way of doing things. One of the main reasons why there are disagreements about the nature of intelligence, as we will see in a moment, or about the number of dimensions which describe personality, is because the number of factors revealed depends on the different factorial techniques used and the number and variety of tests which an investigator subjects to factor analysis. Other difficulties concern the labelling of factors once we have obtained them. Factor analysis exposes the myth that science is objective and neutral.

So let's return to the issue raised at the beginning of this chapter of 'what is intelligence?' One way of answering the question is to analyse the results of IQ tests by such statistical techniques as correlation and factor analyses so as to ascertain the nature of the cognitive abilities that have been measured. The results of the analysis give us a psychometric model or a structure of the intellect. In particular, such a method allows us to examine the *dimensionality* of intelligence; that is whether intelligence is best conceived of as a single dimension along which all individuals can be placed, or whether there are two or more dimensions, such that an individual can be good at one aspect of intelligence and less good at another. A number of different theories or models have been put forward by different investigators. But note that the theories are the result of tests (which is why they are called psychometric). Note, too, that the names given to the parts, dimensions or factors of the theories are labels attached to these factors by the investigators and are the results of factor analysis. The labels should not be reified as some sort of entities.

Spearman's two-factor theory   Charles Spearman was not only an eminent psychologist, but also a fine statistician. In the early 1900s, when correlation coefficients were an exciting new break-through in statistics, Spearman was giving various tests of mental ability to children. What could be more natural for Spearman than to correlate the resulting scores? This would permit him to see how far a particular sub-test score agreed with all other sub-test scores. What he discovered was that each score was positively correlated. In other words, a child with a high score on one sub-test tended to score highly on another. Spearman concluded that all the tests had something in common and this general factor he labelled g for 'general intelligence'. Further, he was convinced that g entered into all intellectual tasks. In addition, Spearman identified 'specific elements' or abilities which he labelled s and which were not highly correlated with each other. Each individual test had a g loading and its own specific loading (s). So the earliest

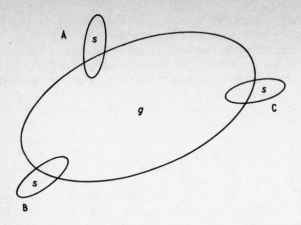

Figure 2 Diagrammatic representation of Spearman's two-factor theory of intelligence.

theory was composed of two factors and may be represented by figure 2.

Spearman's theory conceptualized intelligence as mainly composed of *g*, which has an influence on just about every activity of life from writing a letter to fixing a car. Individuals differ according to how much *g* they possess – bright people having lots, duller people having less; *g* explains why people good at one mental ability also tend to be good at most others. And yet, people also differ according to their specific abilities (*s*) such that one person is better at composing a letter than fixing a car, despite the fact that these activities are to some extent loaded with, or under the control of, *g*, and so are correlated.

Hierarchical theory   This second view has been popular with British psychologists, particularly Cyril Burt and Philip Vernon. Using factor-analytic techniques, just as Spearman had done, Burt established that to conceive of intelligence as composed of *g* and *s* was too simple. He agreed that there is a general ability factor, common to all tests, but also a series of group factors. The number of group factors one establishes depends on the number and variety of tests, but four factors regularly appear in factor analyses – verbal, arithmetical, spatial and mechanical.

At first glance, Burt's hierarchical theory may seem to challenge Spearman's two-factor theory. In fact, it provided an extension and improvement that Spearman later welcomed. Burt's group factors preserved the notion of a hierarchy. It merely added another level between *g* and *s*. In addition, Burt and Spearman agreed that *g* was inherited, dominant and unchangeable while *s* was a function of training. Burt considered that his group factors were also the result of education. Next on to the scene was Thurstone, an American, to attack the hierarchical theory of intellect of the British researchers, though not to oppose the hereditarian claims.

Thurstone's multiple-factor theory   Thurstone, like Spearman and Burt, used factor analysis of test results to investigate the structure of intelligence. But he used a different form of factor analysis and found a very different structure. His theory conceives of intelligence as composed of a number of 'primary mental abilities' (PMAs). The basic model included seven PMAs, with none being more important than another and with no general intelligence factor. The primary abilities include verbal comprehension (the ability to understand the meaning of words), perceptual speed (the ability to grasp visual details quickly), number (the ability to compute numbers), and so on.

The arguments between Thurstone and Spearman–Burt essentially revolve around factor analysis, and we will not go into the finer points here. Thurstone agreed that factor analysis should be used to seek to uncover the real aspects or vectors of mind. It is just that he chose a rather different form of factor analysis. Spearman and Burt chose 'principal component' solutions. Thurstone chose 'simple structure' solutions. The two solutions are mathematically equivalent. Neither is better. All that happens is that the same information is presented in a different form. Which method you choose depends on what you believe is the real nature of intelligence. Thurstone's simple structure gave him primary mental abilities or vectors of mind. Spearman's principal components gave him dominant general intelligence and specific abilities.

Later, Thurstone was forced to admit a certain amount of defeat. A 'second order' factor analysis (applying a second analysis to the results of the first) showed that *g* seemed to be involved in all PMAs. So we are back to the hierarchical theory. Yet the implications of the debate are not confined to mathematics and tests. There are educational and political implications. Gould (1981) puts it eloquently and is worth quoting at length:

23

With Spearman's *g*, each child can be ranked on a single scale of innate intelligence; all else is subsidiary. General ability can be measured early in life and children can be sorted according to their intellectual promise (as in the 11 + examination).

With Thurstone's PMAs, there is no general ability to measure. Some children are good at some things, others excel in different and independent qualities of mind. . . .

From the midst of an economic depression that reduced many of its intellectual elite to poverty, an America with egalitarian ideals (however rarely practised) challenged Britain's traditional equation of social class with innate worth. Spearman's *g* had been rotated away, and general mental worth evaporated with it. (Gould, 1981, p. 304)

Other multiple-factor theories Guilford's theory is also a multiple-factor theory, but instead of seven factors, he maintains that there are at least 120 unique intellectual abilities. He puts forward the view that previous theories do considerable injustice to the richness and variety of intelligence. Guilford analyses intellectual functioning in terms of five mental operations (including thinking, memory and evaluating), six products of these operations (such as classes, relations and transformations) and four types of content upon which operations are performed (figural, symbolic, semantic and behavioural). These classifications yield 120 distinguishable abilities, and a test is being devised for each. We await completion of the project, though Guilford's ideas on two operations, divergent and convergent production, have contributed greatly to work on creativity (see chapter 4).

Finally, Cattell's theory suggests that the general ability (*g*) factor that emerges from most studies that correlate cognitive tests consists of two components – fluid intelligence and crystallized intelligence. Fluid intelligence is a measure of the influence of biological factors and is comparable to inherited ability. Thus it is free from the influence of the culture, education and experience. Crystallized intelligence represents acquired abilities which we have developed under the influence of our cultural environment, our experiences and our education.

Criticisms of factorial models of psychometric intelligence While the idea of intelligence as something measurable, and the whole paraphernalia of testing techniques, have a large body of advocates and followers, they also have many critics. The criticisms are at many levels.

First, there is factor analysis. Most people now agree that the usefulness of factor analysis as a technique for defining the concept of intelligence is severely limited. There are many reasons for this. As we have already seen in the Thurstone–Burt debate, the same data from the same population can give us a number of different patterns of factors, depending on the form of factor analysis used and on decisions concerning the rotation of factors axes. Knowing when to stop the factor analysis is also a problem. A large number of intercorrelations may mean a large number of factors with small loadings on test items. What meaning, if any, do these factors have? We can never know which is the 'correct' model of intelligence since that depends on how we factor-analyse our IQ data.

Secondly, naming a factor is also a difficulty. The normal process is to label it according to the characteristics of the tests which have a high loading on (i.e. are closely related to) the factor. Obviously, this is a highly subjective process, influenced by the preferences of and theories held by the particular researcher. It does not give us an objective psychological definition of structure. If we do not stick with the same data, but add more, the difficulties become worse. This is because the pattern of factors depends on the number and type of tests used, and on the nature of the respondents of the tests. A few, homogenous tests used on subjects who vary widely in age, education and cognitive abilities are likely to result in our factor analysis emphasizing one dominant general ability factor rather than a number of independent, specific factors. On the other hand, a large number of different types of test and a homogenous sample are likely to yield a larger number of independent factors without a clear overall ability factor. How can factor analysis claim to elucidate the psychological structure of intelligence if its results are so dependent on the nature of the sample and the test questions?

Finally, there is the trap of reification. Just because we have labelled a factor 'verbal ability' or 'memory' doesn't mean it 'exists' in any objective sense. A factor is merely a statistic. It doesn't have an identity like a table or chair. Its label is a scientific concept, and yet naming a factor easily leads us to believe, if we are not very careful, that it is something objective.

A more fundamental criticism strikes at the whole notion of intelligence as measurable, at the psychometric tradition itself, in other words. This line of approach criticizes the reliance on tests and statistics to describe a person at a particular point in time. It is pointed out that this reduces the complexity, variety and essential humanness of a person to a single number. That number, an IQ score, encourages an overly narrow view of skills and abilities and ignores the many talents and skills which are not tested. Worse, this number is used to predict and even shape the future of an individual. Examples of such prediction would be the use of IQ scores for occupational purposes such as selecting someone for a job or a training scheme, or educational purposes such as deciding on the type of school for a child at an eleven-plus examination. Such classifying and predicting is seen as being especially dis-advantageous to racial and ethnic minorities, slow learners and mentally handicapped children and adults. Tests place a mark of inferiority on those who do badly which may affect their feelings of self-worth or self-esteem, as well as their future educational or occupational lives. There is also a worrying self-fulfilling proph-ecy about all this. If teachers, parents and the child form certain expectations of his or her school performance, based on an IQ score, this might lead the child to do as well or as badly as everyone expects. Moreover, there is intriguing experimental evidence from the classroom to show that this can happen (Rosenthal and Jacobson, 1968). At the beginning of a school year, certain teachers were told that twenty children in their classes had high IQs, were 'late bloomers' intellectually, and so were expected to do well in the year ahead. In fact, the teachers were deliberately misled. The children were all of average IQ. Yet, sure enough, by the end of the year the twenty children had done very well. The teachers' expectations of the children's superior performance led to the performance they expected. Expectations of 'brightness' led to enthusiasm, interest and affection from the teachers. The children apparently responded by performing up to their best. However, the study was poorly designed: the results are difficult to interpret and it is unwise to place great store by them.

An even wider criticism of testing comes from a more socio-logical point of view. This view sees testing as part of the social process of discrimination. It is said that the use of tests by an individual tester, or by a society which approves of testing, reveals that person's or society's ideologies and values. It emphasizes one person's position of power and influence over another. It dif-ferentiates one person from another. It legitimizes classification procedures. The result is often alienation. A similar position is taken by phenomenologists. They state that there is no such thing as an 'objective' test. Psychometricians view tests as objective and predictive, and testers as detached and relatively passive. Phenomenologists, on the other hand, argue that evaluation should be 'natural', active and open to subjective impressions and intuition, since all data are personal reconstructions determined by our purposes, intentions, values and ideologies.

Philip Vernon, one of the big names in the psychometrics of intelligence, devotes a chapter of his book *Intelligence: Heredity and Environment* (1979) to reviewing criticisms of intelligence tests, and puts forward a defence.

Qualitative or developmental approaches to intelligence

A very different approach to intelligence is the qualitative one. It is not really concerned with the quantitative, psychometric aspects of intelligence that we have just discussed. Instead, it is interested in the nature of intellectual functioning and the development of the intellect. It is concerned, then, with processes rather than with ways in which individuals differ. Therefore we will not spend time discussing this approach here, merely state the fact that this important area of work on intelligence exists. Piaget has done more to further our understanding of these processes than anyone else. In particular, he has been interested in how logical thinking develops, and describes a number of stages from birth to maturity through which this process proceeds. Full details can be found in another book in this series (Turner, 1984) and in Piaget (1954).

More recent cognitive and psychophysiological approaches to intelligence

A third approach to measuring intelligence does not depend directly on classical intelligence tests and their factor structure, nor is it confined to examining the developmental stages of young children. It is based on psychophysiological measurements. Ironically, this is just where it started in the late 1800s, with Galton, and it involves methods which Binet rejected for his measures of reasoning.

The first physiological measure to be investigated by Galton was reaction time (RT), and it continues to be examined by modern psychologists. It is a less direct test of psychophysiological and cortical function than later methods, does not involve complex cognitive processes like IQ tests, and is relatively culture-free.

Only recently have well-designed and controlled studies been conducted which have sought correlations between RT and IQ. There are lots of ways of testing such a relationship. One way is based on the fact that multiple-choice RT increases as a linear function of the increase in amount of information. In other words, when someone is asked to make a choice or decision between two or more bits of information, the time taken to respond (RT) increases as the number of bits of information increases. Many investigators have shown that this relationship correlates with IQ. The increase in RT with greater choice is steeper for low-IQ than for high-IQ subjects.

A second method of using RT to measure IQ is through both short-term and long-term memory experiments. In a short-term memory task of this type, a subject is shown a series of up to seven digits or letters for several seconds. Then another digit is presented, called a 'probe', and the subject is asked to indicate as quickly as possible whether the probe was or was not among the original series. Obviously the speed of the subject's scanning of short-term memory for information is being measured here. Results show that both the simple RT itself and the slope of RT as a function of the number of digits in the series correlates with IQ.

Thirdly, inspection time as a form of RT is related to IQ. A subject is shown a visual stimulus composed of two lines, one longer than the other. A tachistoscope is used to expose the stimulus for a very brief time. Subjects are asked to say whether the longer line was to the right or the left of the short line. Inspection time is increased or decreased so that the subject makes a correct judgement in at least 19 out of 20 trials. RT here is the time needed to inspect a visual stimulus so that a correct decision can be made. Correlations between RT and IQ range from -0.31 for highly homogenous samples to -0.80 for highly heterogenous samples. In other words, subjects with high IQ tend to need less time to make a correct decision than do low-IQ subjects. (See Jensen, 1981, for a more detailed review of RT and IQ, and Brand and Deary, 1982, for a review of inspection time and IQ.)

Many of the studies in this tradition show high and consistent relationships between RT and IQ. Since RT is, as far as we know, not affected by culture or education, we may be approaching a culture-free measure of IQ. At least, that is what most of the investigators in this area claim.

It is possible that the results of other work on IQ and psychophysiology, such as electroencephalographs (EEGs) and IQ, might also be leading towards a 'purer' measure of intelligence. EEGs are records of the electrical activity made by the brain and are obtained when electrodes are temporarily fixed to the scalp. When visual or auditory stimuli are suddenly presented to the subject, a particular wave feature known as the averaged evoked potential (AEP) is obtained, and appears on the paper record as a large spiky formation following and preceding the normal, flatter, more gentle wave formation characteristic of the resting state of a person. Investigators have shown that the AEP latencies (i.e. the length of time in milliseconds that the wave form lasts) and the amplitude of the AEP are correlated with IQ. Latencies tend to be longer for low-IQ than for high-IQ subjects, a negative correlation, while amplitude is positively correlated. The correlations are not high, usually less than 0.5 and replications of the work have not always been successful. An early investigator in this field was Ertl (Ertl, 1971; Ertl and Schafer, 1969) who, according to Kamin (Eysenck versus Kamin, 1981), was the president of a business firm that attempted to sell 'brain wave analyzers' to school systems as a culture-free intelligence test, and was, furthermore, unable to repeat his early results. Hardly a testimony to rigorous and objective scientific endeavour!

Lately, though, work at the Maudsley Hospital, London (Hendrickson and Hendrickson, 1980) has yielded much higher correlations between AEP and IQ. Why, though, should such correlations exist? What is the meaning of this composite AEP/IQ relationship? The theoretical interpretation put forward by the Hendricksons is extremely complicated and controversial, but is based on a 'pulse-train' hypothesis resembling the ways in which computers work. They put forward the view that the high-IQ subject's distinctive AEP is associated with the subject running through similar mental processes to those of the low-IQ subjects, but with fewer neural errors. It could also be that these results tie in with the inspection-time work, to yield an explanation in terms of the simple idea of mental speed.

Later work might confirm the findings of the Hendricksons, although work by Rust (1975) failed to find any correlation between evoked potential and IQ. If the exploratory studies are confirmed, together with other work with RT and inspection time, this will open up some exciting possibilities, including many practical, social and political implications. Physiological measures of IQ might allow much more rigorous and fair testing of varying age, socio-economic, national, ethnic and racial groups. We await developments.

Conclusion

Quite some time has been spent on reviewing the factorial, qualitative and (more recent) cognitive/psychophysiological approaches to studying intelligence. By now the reader may see the force of what was said at the outset of this chapter, namely that the concept of intelligence varies and is difficult to pin down. Perhaps the work linking intelligence-test performance and such measures as inspection time offers one way out of this impasse. If we are having difficulty with the concept of intelligence, maybe we could dispense with it altogether and talk instead in terms of an individual's information-processing capacity. The model of human beings as information processors, borrowing heavily from ideas in engineering and cybernetics, has proved very useful indeed in the development of theories of memory. Thus, instead of testing a person's 'intelligence', we might assess his or her ability to receive, encode, store (in short-term or long-term memory) and retrieve information. Inspection time is an example of a measure of one aspect of this process. Will psychologists jettison the vague and elusive notion of intelligence in favour of the more complex but potentially precise information-processing model? If they do, they will bring this area of study right back into the mainstream of experimental psychology. Whether it will happen is too early to say, though it is hard to imagine the lay use of the term 'intelligence' dying out.

The nature–nurture debate

The nature–nurture debate regarding intelligence has raged between psychologists ever since the concept of IQ was introduced. On the one hand, there are some who believe that IQ is determined totally by environment. Kamin (1977) says that 'There exists no data which should lead a prudent man to accept the hypothesis that IQ test scores are in any degree heritable.' Or, putting it another way, that the 'data cannot even establish that the heritability of IQ is significantly greater than zero' (Eysenck versus Kamin, 1981, p. 104). Hereditarians, on the other hand, deny the importance of environment as an explanation of differences in IQ. Eysenck is usually seen as the main British proponent of the hereditarian position, though as Rawles (1981) points out:

> Eysenck . . . is an 'interactionist', or more precisely and neologistically an 'additivist' who argues that the relative contributions of heredity and environment to the production of IQ variation within a population are open to estimation by the gathering of experimental observations and their subjection to various statistical and model building procedures.

Note the phrase 'relative contributions of heredity and environment'. This is the essence of the nature–nurture debate. How important are the contributions of heredity and environment to producing IQ? Kamin seems to think environment contributes 100 per cent. Eysenck thinks heredity contributes 80 per cent and environment 20 per cent. Most people agree that the differences observed in intelligence are the result of the *interaction* of the two elements, but what relative part do each play? In order to attempt to answer the question, let's examine the evidence.

Twin studies

A good method of investigation, according to hereditarians, is twin studies. There are two types of twin, monozygotic (MZ) or identical twins and dizygotic (DZ) or fraternal twins. MZ twins derive from the same fertilized ovum and therefore have identical genes. DZ twins derive from two separate fertilized ova and are no more alike genetically than siblings (ordinary brothers and sisters). When IQ measurements are made of both types of twin, then the extent to which MZ twins have a closer correlation of scores than do DZ twins can be taken as an indication of the genetic contribution. Typical of work in this tradition is an early study in Britain by Herrman and Hogben (1932) which showed that for 65 pairs of MZ twins the mean difference in IQ was 9.2, while for the 96 DZ twins of the same sex it was 17.7, and for siblings it was 16.8. This shows, first, that there is very little difference between the scores of DZ and ordinary siblings, suggesting that twins are not treated differently from ordinary siblings in ways that might affect intelligence. Yet there is a reasonably large difference between the scores of MZ and DZ twins. Since MZ twins have identical genes and DZ twins do not, we can conclude that genetic influences cause their greater IQ similarity. There have been very many studies comparing MZ and DZ twins, and invariably they report higher IQ correlations of MZ than of DZ twins. Typically, the correlations for the MZ twins range from about 0.70 to 0.90 and for DZ same-sex twins from about 0.50 to 0.70. In the Herrman and Hogben study it was 0.84 and 0.53 respectively. There is no doubt that MZ correlations are higher than DZ correlations. The problem is, what does it mean?

Hereditarians say it is due to the greater genetic similarity of MZ twins. Environmentalists disagree. They point out that the home, school and general social environment for a pair of MZ twins is likely to be much more alike than is the environment for DZ twins. For the most part, this is for the obvious reason that MZ twins usually look strikingly alike. So parents, teachers, relatives and friends will treat them alike. They are also likely to spend time together, play together, have friends in common, dress alike and sleep in the same room. Even in middle age, MZ twins say that they see each other much more often than do DZ twins. There is some evidence, though not much, that MZ twins who are more alike physically, have IQs that are more alike. This, say the environmentalists, shows that it is environment – physical resemblance causing them to have similar experience – that explains the MZ and DZ IQ findings. It is not the result of genetics.

The hereditarians' next thrust is as follows. We agree, they say, that environment plays a part in the MZ and DZ IQ findings. The fact that the typical IQ correlation for a group of MZ twins is around 0.80 shows this. If it were *wholly* genetics, that figure would be 1.0, since MZ twins are identical genetically. The difference between 0.8 and 1.0 leaves a lot of room for environmental influences. But the environmental reasons of looking alike, being treated alike and behaving alike do not account for the bulk of the difference. It just doesn't account for *enough* of the difference to rule out the conclusion of approximately an 80 per cent role played by genetics and a 20 per cent role played by the environment. (It should be noted that not all hereditarians subscribe to the 80–20 per cent rule. But Eysenck and Jensen, the two leading proponents, do.) Anyway, there are lots of ways of examining the relative roles of heredity and environment. It is the *accumulation* of the findings supporting the hereditarians (say the hereditarians) that makes their position so strong.

Another way is to look at studies of MZ twins reared apart. These studies are particularly important and interesting because they seem to provide information on individuals with identical heredity but different environments. They can be compared with DZ twins and siblings who have rather different heredities but the same, or rather, similar, environments and with MZ twins reared together, who have identical heredities and a more similar environment than MZs brought up separately. Not only are cases of MZ twins reared apart important, they are also very rare. Many of us might agree with the following:

> If I had any desire to lead a life of indolent ease, I would wish to be an identical twin, separated at birth from my brother and raised in a different social class. We could hire ourselves out to a host of social scientists and practically name our fee. For we would be exceedingly rare representatives of the only adequate natural experiment for separating genetic from environmental effects in humans – genetically identical individuals raised in disparate environments. (Gould, 1981, p. 234)

Only four major studies have been reported, and one of these was by Cyril Burt. There are now considerable doubts about the genuineness of Burt's data (Hearnshaw, 1979) and so his results are best discarded. The remaining three studies are summarized in table 2, and it can be seen that, so rare are separated MZ twins, that only sixty-nine cases have been reported.

The average correlation of 0.74 compares with around 0.80 for MZs reared together and 0.60 for DZs reared together. So identical twins reared apart are more similar in IQ than fraternal twins reared together. It seems unlikely that identical twins reared apart should have a *more* similar environment than fraternal twins reared together. Certainly environment plays a part because the MZs reared together are more similar than MZs reared apart. It would seem, though, that genetics plays a large part in IQ, and environment a much smaller part.

Not so, say the environmentalists. There are numerous reasons why these studies provide no unambiguous evidence for the

Table 2 Intraclass correlations between MZ twins reared apart. (After Vernon, 1979, p. 170)

Study	Number of cases		Correlation coefficient
Newman *et al.* (1937)	19		0.67
Shields (1962)	38		0.78
Juel-Nielsen (1965)	12		0.68
Total	69	Weighted average	0.74

heritability of IQ. The primary reason is that these twins are not truly separated. The environments to which they went are highly correlated. Some were reared by relatives. Others were separated in such a way that the mother kept one and the other went to close family friends. Others were brought up just a few hundred yards from each other, played a lot together and went to the same school. Some had not been separated until the age of 7 or later. In the Shields study (1962), the requirement to be counted as a separate twin pair was merely that the children had been reared in different homes for at least five years sometime in their childhoods. It is very difficult to say that any of the Shields twins were reared in very different social conditions.

Other criticisms have been made of these studies. One is of unconscious bias. In all three studies the same experimenter tested the IQs of the majority of *both* twins. It was not a 'blind' experiment. It is well known in psychology that the values, theories and wishes of experimenters can *unconsciously* influence the behaviour of the subjects and the recording of data. It is possible that this unconscious bias on the part of the IQ tester could have artificially inflated the IQ correlation of the twins, since the tester would have known both sets of results. Other criticisms have been levelled at these studies, including defective standardization of tests, the fact that twins are not a representative sample of the population and the volunteer-subjects issue – the fact that the twins may not be a representative sample of all separated twins. (A very readable account of the environmental view of twin studies can be found in a book by Oliver Gillie, 1976, the medical correspondent of the *Sunday Times* who exposed the Burt fraud.) The question remains. Are these criticisms strong enough and plausible enough to account for the observed differences?

Foster-child studies

We cannot leave this fascinating squabble without mentioning one other block of evidence. This is foster-child studies. We can compare the IQ differences between a fostered child and his or her natural parents, on the one hand, and his or her foster parents on the other. If heredity is more important, the correlation between child and natural parents should be higher than between child and foster parent. If home environment is more important, the difference should be the other way round. Unlike the work on separated MZ twins, in this area of study we are not handicapped by lack of subjects. Studies reporting data on well over 1000 pairs of children have been reported. The median correlation between foster child and foster parents is around 0.20, slightly higher for foster mothers and lower for foster fathers. This might be taken, crudely, as the environmental component. The median correlation for foster children and natural parent(s) is around 0.30, which might be taken as the genetic component. The correlation for natural parents and their children reared with them is around 0.50. Apparently, then, home environment is of importance, though less so than heredity.

Similar to these studies are those of children adopted shortly after birth. A number of studies have been reported and they again suggest a high heritability component to IQ. Eysenck puts the figure at 64 per cent for these studies (Eysenck versus Kamin, 1981). Hereditarians say that these results make it difficult to deny the strong genetic component of IQ.

Not so, say the environmentalists. For one thing, the earlier studies upon which the hereditarians base their case are suspect. There are two major flaws. One is selective placement. The suggestion is that when adoption agencies place a child, they try to fit the child to the home. Children from bright and well-educated mothers might be placed in 'good' homes, with high-IQ foster parents. Children who appear less bright or who come from homes with less bright or less well-educated mothers might be placed in less favourable environments, even though the homes are still 'good' ones. This is selective placement. Kamin (1977) cites evidence that it is often practised by adoption agencies and it is this that could conceivably account for the correlation between the IQ of the natural mother and that of her adopted or fostered child, even if she has never lived with the child.

The second flow is more technical and is due to the restricted variance in adoptive families. Foster or adoption homes are likely to provide a much better than average home for children. For one thing, foster parents actively want a child, which is not always true of biological parents. Agencies are also very careful about who they allow to foster or adopt. Those wanting to foster must be sufficiently well off, financially secure, emotionally stable, not alcoholic, have no criminal record, and so on. This restricted variance means that the correlation between foster parents and adopted child's IQ will tend to be artificially depressed. The point may be made clearer by the following quote:

To understand this technical point, consider the correlation between a man's weight and his success as a boxer. It would be very high if boxers of all weights were allowed to fight each other because the heavyweight boxer would almost always defeat the lightweight. To avoid such a correlation, definite weight divisions have been established by boxing authorities. Fights can only take place between boxers of reasonably similar weight, and the correlation between weight and boxing success is consequently very low. We are suggesting that in terms of the environments provided for their children almost all adoptive parents – unlike biological parents – are in the heavyweight division. (Kamin, in Eysenck versus Kamin, 1981, p. 117)

The final environmentalist reason for rejection of the hereditarian case based on foster-children data is that some studies show the power of the environment in determining IQ. A recent study is by Schiff *et al.* (1978) in France. They report data on thirty-two children born to parents of low socio-economic status (SES) and adopted at less than 6 months of age by parents of high SES. They compared these children's IQ with that of their real (biological) siblings who had been reared by their own mothers. Note, then, that the genetic component is held constant, and the only thing to vary is home environment. The adopted children had an average IQ of 111, while the stay-with-mother children had an average of 95: strong evidence for the power of a 'good' home.

Conclusion

Where does all this apparently conflicting evidence get us? One thing that can be said is that it should make us cautious. We must remind ourselves that cognitive ability is a complex phenomenon, too complex to be totally measurable by a single number called 'IQ'. We cannot know for certain the respective roles of heredity and environment, of nature and of nurture, in an IQ score. Intelligence is determined by a complex interaction of the two components. To some, the fact that the two are so inextricably bound together in a mutually reinforcing process makes the question of how much each contributes to intelligence a meaningless one to ask. These pragmatic people argue that we should just be concerned to develop whatever ability a person has as far as their innate inheritance allows. To others, the question is of great theoretical and practical importance. It is of practical importance because evaluation of social policy, such as the eleven-plus examination, teaching methods, and programmes aimed at improving the abilities of the disadvantaged hinge on whether or not intelligence is substantially modifiable by environmental changes. To some the question may be an important one, but they view it as impossible to answer. To others, it is answerable by recourse to the sorts of study reported in this chapter.

If you believe it is important, and it is answerable, what can you conclude? That is the most difficult question of all, and the one requiring the most caution. Almost certainly, both heredity and environment play a part in IQ. The cumulative effect of the different sorts of study (and some, such as animal studies, not reported here) makes it highly unlikely that intelligence is determined solely by environment as Kamin would have us believe. It may possibly be that genetics is a rather more important factor, but if IQ differences are due to genetic factors they are still modifiable by the environment. Even though differences in height have a genetic component of around 1.0, the height of the British and American populations has increased by some inches in the past hundred years due, presumably, to improvements in health, hygiene and nutrition. In the case of the Japanese the increase has been as much as two inches in the past twenty years. Finally, genetic causation of intelligence *within* a population allows nothing necessarily to be said about genetic causation of intelligence differences *between* two populations. It is to this debate that we turn in chapter 8, when we discuss racial differences in intelligence.

4 Creativity

Creativity is obviously an important element in individual differences. If we look back in history, we can see that the world we live in has been radically altered by a few individuals who have made creative leaps forward in their thinking. Galileo, Darwin and Einstein made enormous contributions to our understanding of the world we live in. Inventions also demonstrate the point: pocket calculators, the telephone, the steam engine and thousands of other items we take for granted have been conceived and developed by people we would want to call 'creative'. In the arts, the books, poems, paintings and sculptures which enrich our world have been produced by highly creative individuals throughout the ages.

Since the 1950s, psychologists have intensified their researches on creativity. The result at the present time is a large body of material which reflects different approaches to the topic and different definitions of the concept of creativity. In order to structure the topic, therefore, we must briefly examine these definitions.

Definitions of 'creativity'

Some definitions of creativity stress that there must be a useful *product* if a person or an act is to be called creative, while other definitions see creativity as valuable in itself without any need for social value. So dreams of the imagination of a child are seen as creative. The examples given earlier of scientific ideas or theories such as the theory of evolution, or products such as the pocket calculator or a classic novel, would fall within the 'socially useful product' definition. The problem with this definition is the level of accomplishment. *How* useful and new must the product be for the originator to be called creative? At an extreme, we may have to say that whole fields of activity are creative, and so all inventors, all painters and all poets from Shakespeare to the lavatory-wall graffiti artist have to be included. Studies in this tradition have taken groups of creative professionals, such as architects and writers, and compared them with people in general to build up a picture of the 'creative person'. But a different picture emerges if we compare very creative architects with less creative architects. For example, architects as a group score much higher than the general population on intelligence, but creative architects do not score higher than architects taken as a whole.

A second set of definitions places 'creativity' more in the psychometric tradition. This approach suggests that creativity (or, rather, divergent thinking, as it is usually called in this context) is an ability that is measurable in ways similar to the measurement of intelligence; that some people are more original than others; and that this type of thinking is different from intelligence-test-type (convergent) thinking. Such an approach focuses more on ability in tests than on achievement in the 'real world'. The important point about the different definitions and approaches to creativity is that research findings may seem confusing or contradictory if we ignore the particular definition of creativity being used and the assumption that this makes about the nature of creativity.

A third approach examines creativity not so much in terms of its products or its measurement, but as an attitude, or a disposition, or a motivation. Vernon approaches creativity in this way. He says: 'the creativity of outstanding artists and scientists is probably more a matter of personality and motivation than just of certain "styles" of thinking' (Vernon, 1979, p. 65). We agree. So let's turn to studies of creative individuals to see what they reveal.

Studies of creative people

One way of studying creativity is to study eminent creative people. The best-known work of this kind has been carried out at the Institute of Personality Assessment and Research in California (see Vernon, 1973). The early work asked a number of professors of architecture to draw up a list of the forty most creative architects in the USA. The names on these lists were matched with other architects of similar age and educational background who were not nominated as creative. In this way, an experimental and a control group were formed and invited to spend a weekend at the Institute taking tests, having interviews and being observed in different situations. All those taking part were male. Comparisons could then be made between the creative and 'not creative' groups. There were considerable differences.

The creative architects had different self-images from those in the control group. They saw themselves as creative, inventive, industrious, independent, individualistic and determined. Those in the control group more often used words such as sincere, reliable, tolerant and responsible. The creative individuals were also closer to the feminine stereotype in our culture by being more open to their own feelings and emotions and expressing interest in such 'feminine' tasks as house-cleaning. Similar studies have also been conducted at the Institute of Personality Assessment and Research of creative writers, mathematicians, engineers, and others, with very similar findings. Other studies have added descriptions such as high energy, attraction to complexity and broad interests, and have shown that such characteristics are often present in the individual from childhood. Moreover, early creative ability is predictive of later creativity. It is well known in psychology that one of the best measures of future behaviour is past behaviour, and the topic of creativity is no exception. Creative adults have often designed, written or created more products as children or young adults, be those products published poems, pieces of music, inventions or whatever, than have less creative people.

There are a number of important points hidden in the list of adjectives cited by the creative architects and others. One is that they *saw* themselves as creative. Research has shown that other creative people see themselves as creative. It may sound very simple and obvious, but one of the best ways of measuring people's creativity is just to ask them if they are creative. You might like to remember this point when in a few pages' time we come to the section on the measurement of creativity.

A second point concerns the independent and individualistic nature of the creative individual. This brings us back to our definition of product-centred creativity. You may remember that we have Galileo and Darwin as obvious examples of creative people. Yet they had to throw aside the conventional wisdom of the time, to take an independent line often in the face of hostility to their new ideas. Creativity, it seems, requires a particular personality. One who has the confidence, independence and determination to strike out on his or her own, to step outside the normal confines of thought.

Finally, the industrious, hard-working element in the creative process often gets overlooked. It has been said that creativity or genius is 10 per cent inspiration and 90 per cent perspiration. This maxim seems to be borne out by the study of creative people and the process of creation. We find in the study of architects, and in many similar studies, that the truly creative individuals are usually devoted to their craft. They work at it harder than others, for longer, and with a dedication bordering on the obsessional. The flash of inspiration, if it comes, is usually preceded by weeks, months or years of perspiration, as we can see in the next section on the process of creation.

The creative process

Another issue which has excited psychologists is the question of how a creative idea is born. Are there recognizable stages in creation? What has to happen before a creative idea takes place? The answer seems to be that there are certain stages that creative people report going through, and that these are very similar for both scientific and artistic endeavours. Full details can be found in Ghiselli (1952), or in a useful summary by Howarth and Gillham (1981), who analyse the process into some key steps.

1 People often say that their creative thought processes are characterized by an inner dialogue. Freud and others have said that this dialogue is between the conscious and the unconscious. Others have given examples of an imaginary dialogue between themselves and some 'other' person. Whoever or whatever the 'other' is, its presence helps the creative process along.

2 Many insights have come while the originator was in a semi-conscious, dream-like state such as we experience between waking and sleeping, or when we observe ourselves doing something without feeling a part of it. Deliberately trying to promote creativity through drug-induced semi-conscious states, though, does not seem to work.

3 At an early stage, when ideas are being formulated, thinkers sometimes report that they avoid using words and conventional logic. Instead they deal in fuzzy images or abstractions. Only later do they put their ideas into words.

4 Finally, there is the considerable concentration, commitment and energy devoted to the creative enterprise, mentioned earlier, especially to laying the groundwork before a creative idea results. Many thinkers report that they submersed themselves for months or years in their chosen endeavour before making a breakthrough. This seems to give the unconscious the material to work on before it can be reordered or recombined into a new insight, idea or product, often when the thinker is not consciously attending to the matter.

Measurement of 'creativity'

There is a whole range of different techniques for assessing creativity, reflecting the many approaches and definitions mentioned at the beginning of this section. A review by Hocevar (1980) looks at ten different approaches, from interest and personality inventories to judgement of products and studies of eminence. But the most widely used approach, and the one we shall concentrate on here, is to describe creativity in terms of divergent thinking and to measure it with tests. Traditional intelligence tests usually require just one answer which is right or wrong. In other words, the test requires the testee's thinking to converge on one solution. In the USA, in the 1950s and 1960s, there was considerable criticism of such tests and of an educational system which was believed to encourage conventional thought and conformity to the authority of the teacher or the textbook. What was needed to help solve the problems of the modern world, like pollution, famine and scarcity of finite resources, was not analytical, convergent thinking but divergent thinking. This emphasizes problem-solving which diverges towards lots of possible solutions and radically new ideas.

Guilford and his colleagues developed tests in the 1950s to

measure divergent thinking, and many similar tests have been developed since. All ask the testee to think of lots of answers to a question, not just one. Questions might be: How many uses can you think of for a brick, or a paperclip? Or: If gravity were suddenly to cease, what would be some of the consequences? Answers can be scored for fluency, which is the number of answers produced, and for flexibility, which is the number of shifts from one sort of use to another. Answers to the paperclip question such as to clean out your ears, to clean your nails, to pick your nose and to clean your navel would get a reasonably high score for fluency but not for flexibility. An answer which went: to clean your nails, to make a fuse, a propellor for a model aircraft, a pipe cleaner and an ear-ring for a punk – would get a higher score for flexibility.

The assumption is that divergent thinking is central to creative problem-solving and that an individual's divergent-thinking test score is a measure of his or her creative thinking. The empirical basis of these assumptions, though, is hard to find and even harder to have faith in. For one thing, the process of creation seems to require both convergent and divergent thinking. A creative individual may need to come up with lots of new possibilities, but may also need to converge on the one which is most suitable or feasible. Secondly, the correlations of divergent-thinking scores with other measures of creativity, such as ratings and products, are inconsistent. Some investigators have found positive relationships, though seldom higher than 0.3, and many others have found no relationship. In other words, the tests lack construct validity – independent evidence that they measure what they claim to measure. Thirdly, even more damaging is the inconclusiveness of evidence that divergent thinking is related to real-life creative problem-solving. What evidence there is suggests that the relationship is far from being one to one and needs substantial qualifications. A review by Barron and Harrington (1981) states: 'Some divergent thinking tests, administered under some conditions and scored by some sets of criteria, do measure abilities related to creative achievement and behaviour in some domains' (Barron and Harrington, 1981, p. 447). At best, divergent thinking should be seen as a correlate of creativity, not as a direct measure of it. Better methods are an inventory of creative activities or accomplishments (where the subject ticks the appropriate ones) or simply asking the subject how creative he or she is.

Finally, there is the problem of whether divergent-thinking tests are different from IQ tests, or whether they are both in fact measuring the same thing. The question has been the subject of many studies. The results show that the correlation of IQ with divergent thinking varies very widely, from zero to 0.7, depending on the nature of the test, the heterogeneity of the sample and the testing situation itself. A figure of about 0.3 is the average correlation. This suggests that divergent-thinking tests measure something different from but related to IQ. But, as we said above, this does not prove that the tests measure creativity. Furthermore, the many tests of divergent thinking only correlate with each other as little (or as much) as they correlate with IQ. This has been taken as casting doubt on the conclusion that we *are* reliably measuring something different. Perhaps we ought to say that the tests might be measuring some things that are different from IQ. Certainly, real-life creativity needs both high intelligence and high 'divergent production', as the studies of creative people show. Whether divergent thinking is a separate factor from intelligence, and whether we are able yet to measure it satisfactorily with divergent-thinking tests, is still very much an open question.

5 Personality

The psychologist's concept of personality is, alas, no easier to define than his or her notion of intelligence; indeed, in some ways it is even more difficult to pin down. Some theorists take personality to mean all the enduring qualities of the individual while others limit their use of the term to observable traits that are not predominantly cognitive in nature – thus excluding such attributes as intelligence and aptitude. There are those working in the field who concentrate on explaining personality in terms of the individual's experience of the world; yet in the writings of other theorists you will find little or no reference to the individual's experience but a great deal of emphasis on his or her behaviour. It follows from this diversity that there is no simple, correct definition of personality; you choose your definition according to your theoretical predilections and, to an extent, the use you are going to make of personality theory. So, if you were inclined towards a Freudian approach, you might want to define personality in such a way that it incorporates some recognition of the role of the unconscious, whereas a behaviourist definition would be couched more in terms of learned, observable behaviours. On the other hand, if you wanted to use personality theory to help you in a specific task, such as understanding the process of occupational choice a young person was going through, you might – given a fairly eclectic outlook – choose whichever theory seemed to make the most sense of the problem before you and afforded the best insight into it.

For our own purposes, we might usefully start by taking a typical, fairly broad definition: 'Personality refers to those relatively stable and enduring aspects of the individual which distinguish him from other people, and at the same time, form the basis of our predictions concerning his future behaviour' (Wright *et al.*, 1970, p. 511). This definition has the virtue of being readily understandable and reasonably wide in scope. But it would still be judged inadequate on some grounds, not least for its reference to 'stable and enduring' qualities. This touches on a debate within personality theory that we will need to consider in some detail. Before we turn to that, however, it is worth pausing to note that the definition given above bears no resemblance to the answer you would get from a layman if you asked what was meant by personality. In everyday language, people are described as having 'a lot of personality' or a 'good personality'. This is usually a way of saying that the person concerned typically exhibits a variety of socially attractive behaviours. In the language of the psychologist it is quite meaningless to talk about anyone having 'more' or 'less' personality. Although individual aspects of personality, like a person's degree of extraversion, may be measured, personality itself is a broad and complex concept that cannot be quantified. Nor is there any question of making moral judgements about what constitutes good or less good personalities, though clearly particular facets of an individual's personality may be more or less socially desirable.

Now, to return to the question of how stable are personality characteristics, most theories assume that individuals possess traits or other qualities that are consistent across different situations and over time (defined by Hall and Lindzey, 1957, as 'a determining tendency or predisposition to respond'). The reader might like to think of this in relation to himself or herself. How consistent are you in your behaviour? Are you extraverted, honest, anxious, etc., in all circumstances? Do you present much the same personality to your friends as to your parents? And have you changed over the past five years or so? The likelihood is that you will see your behaviour changing quite a lot from situation to situation. In fact, when asked to explain our behaviour, we tend to attribute it to various aspects of the circumstances in which it took place. But when asked to explain somebody else's behaviour, we have a strong inclination to explain it in terms of their characteristic behaviour, their personality. This is what is sometimes called 'the fundamental attribution error' (Ross, 1977). Much of our perception of the world is an attempt to cut down its enormous complexity to something our cognitive capabilities can handle. This means simplifying objects and events by categorizing them. Our perceptions of other people are no different in this respect – we reduce the complexity of their behaviour by making dispositional attributions, that is we explain their actions by reference to internal dispositions ('That's typical of her, she's such a generous person'; 'Well, what do you expect of someone as selfish as him?'). But when it comes to explaining our own behaviour, we suddenly feel the urge to adopt a more sophisticated level of analysis, one that involves situational factors as well!

Is there no more consistency in personality than the amount we impose on our perceptions of it to make things simpler? That was the implication of Mischel's (1968) attack on the trait approach, in which he claimed that behaviour is largely determined by situational variables rather than by internal, dispositional influences. Supporting this, Mischel produced evidence that there was only a rather low correlation (around 0.2 to 0.3) between measures of personality and actual behaviour that was supposed to be reflected by those measures. Plenty of other studies illustrate the importance of the individual's situation. For example, Latané and Darley (1970) showed that people were less likely to report a crime if others had witnessed it than if they had witnessed it alone. Mischel's advocacy of 'situationalism' in opposition to the established notions about personality has a lot in common with the nature versus nurture debate on intelligence; there is an implication that if behaviour is primarily situationally determined, then 'personality' is an almost infinitely malleable thing.

This approach has drawn a typically robust reply from Eysenck (Eysenck and Eysenck, 1980), echoed by Kline (1983). The substance of their counter-argument is empirical, quoting studies that show consistency between ratings and questionnaire data and behaviour, with correlations around 0.80. For example, Epstein (1979) studied his subjects' behaviour over several weeks. The relationship between self-rating of mood and subjects' physiological reactions and quality of task performance was found to be strongly positive when looked at over a long period. This contrasts with much of the evidence quoted by Mischel in which one personality measure would be correlated with a single short test of behaviour in a laboratory, or some similar kind of very limited comparison was carried out. As ever, the truth probably lies in between the two points of view. The *interactionist* perspective (Endler, 1975) emphasizes the importance of the mutual influence of situational and dispositional variables. To fail to take both sides of the equation into account would seem to be flying in the face of both the evidence and common sense. The trait theorists have always acknowledged – though perhaps not adequately – the impact of situational variables, and Mischel (1977) in his later writings seems to have moved to a more interactionist position.

There are many other issues and problems that beset personality theories, but we will mention just one more for the moment. This is the difference in perspective between those who espouse an *idiographic* view of personality and those who favour a *nomothetic* approach to the subject. The idiographic theorist, such as Gordon Allport, emphasizes the uniqueness of each personality and concentrates on the study of the pattern of interacting variables in individuals, while the nomothetic theorist focuses on the ways in which personalities are alike and can be compared. Eysenck (1952a), for example, says 'to the scientists, the unique individual is simply the point of intersection of a number of quantitative variables'. The psychologist working in the applied field needs both approaches. For instance, a clinician faced with understanding a patient's problem will often often it helpful to know how this person stands relative to his or her peers in terms of such things as intelligence, sociability, anxiety, and so on. But the clinician will also have to understand how these and many other physical, psychological and environmental variables interact to produce this particular personality. There may well be general laws relating to this too, but it seems unlikely that they can ever be formulated to such an extent as to cover all the possible permutations and combinations of such variables. Allport (1961, p. 12) comes to the following well-judged conclusion: 'There is no reason why we should not learn from every generalization about human nature that we can. At the same time we need to be alert to concepts and methods that enable us to understand patterned individuality.'

Now that we have considered the use of the term 'personality' and touched on some of the different viewpoints to be found in this field, we can move on to look at the theories themselves. Most books on individual differences understandably concentrate on nomothetic theories, as these are the ones that most readily facilitate direct and measurable comparisons between individuals, and as such they are very much in keeping with this area of psychology. However, they cannot really be evaluated in isolation and need to be seen against the background of other, sometimes more idiographic approaches. So, in this chapter, while most of the space will be devoted to the nomothetically orientated theories of Eysenck and Cattell, we will also look at a striking example of an idiographic theory, namely Kelly's personal construct theory. As the earlier 'depth' theories of personality were discussed in chapter 2, they will not be repeated here – but they should certainly not be forgotten.

Eysenck's theory

H.J. Eysenck is almost certainly the best-known British psychologist, chiefly through his prodigious output of books and papers, many of the former being written for the general public in an exceptionally clear and interesting way. He has not been backward in coming forward and has appeared in various media to expound his views in his own inimitable style. His theories, particularly in relation to the hereditability of characteristics like intelligence, and what might be described as his very self-confident manner of putting them across and of dealing with his critics, have not always won him friends.

Eysenck's studies started (Eysenck, 1947) with a factor analysis of rating-scale data obtained on 700 servicemen diagnosed as neurotics. He used a second-order factorization (see p. 23), and from it identified two factors, neuroticism and introversion–extraversion. Neuroticism – or emotionality, as Eysenck sometimes calls it – is characterized by such things as a tendency to worry, various physical symptoms associated with anxiety and an unstable mood state. The opposite end of this continuum is emotional stability. His notion of extraversion seems to consist of two primary components, namely sociability and impulsivity; the highly extraverted individual is cheerful, friendly, spontaneous, active and expressive, and the introverted person presents the opposite picture (aloof, inhibited, etc.). Later studies using a variety of populations, including normal individuals, confirmed the existence of these two major dimensions of personality. As extraversion and neuroticism are assumed to be normally distributed, most people would be placed around the middle of these continua and thus fall between the extremes.

Eysenck's later factor-analytic studies yielded two other dimensions of personality, intelligence and psychoticism. Although he has recently done a good deal of work on the concept of intelligence (as we saw in chapter 3), this has not been discussed in any great depth in his writings on personality as such. His psychoticism dimension has been the most controversial of all. In effect, Eysenck is suggesting that there is no qualitative difference between normal and psychotic individuals, only a quantitative one, and that there is thus a continuity between the extreme behaviour of the psychotic and the behaviour of the normal individual. The person high in psychoticism seems to be cruel, lacking in feeling, aggressive, careless of danger and solitary, amongst other things. In contrast to the distribution on the other dimensions, on psychoticism it is highly skewed, with the vast majority of people being very low on this attribute (Eysenck and Eysenck, 1976).

Eysenck (1963) postulates a biological basis for dimensions of personality, with the attendant implication of a strong hereditary influence in their determination. The theory suggests that individuals inherit a particular type of nervous system that predisposes them in one direction or another, the final 'shape' of the personality being determined by the interaction between the person's biological predisposition and the environmental conditions encountered. In the case of extraversion – introversion, the position of an individual rests in the first instance on the balance between excitation and inhibition processes within the central nervous system, and more specifically on the reticular activating system (RAS). The RAS is located in the central core of the brainstem and has as a primary purpose the maintenance of an optimum level of alertness for the individual. In achieving this, it can either boost the transmission of incoming sensory data to the cortex through excitation of the neural impulses or it can 'damp down' the transmission through the inhibition of these impulses. Eysenck says that extraverts have 'strong' nervous systems – they have a bias in the RAS towards inhibition of neural impulses; inhibition builds up strongly and quickly, thus reducing the intensity of any sensory stimulation of the cortex. For introverts, the bias is in the other direction; they have 'weak' nervous systems, with the RAS providing weak inhibition and strong excitation (or boosting) of incoming sensory stimulation, thereby amplifying its intensity.

Putting this another way, albeit rather crudely, for extraverts it may take a lot of stimulation to make any impact (hence the fact that they are 'stimulus-hungry') while for the introvert a little stimulation will go a long way.

It does not take any great leap to see that this hypothesized difference would influence conditionability. Introverts, because of their sensory sensitivity, will condition rapidly and strongly, while extraverts will form conditioned responses slowly and weakly (unless the stimuli involved are presented frequently and at a high intensity). This difference in conditionability is in turn part of the explanation for the characteristically different patterns of behaviour shown by introverts and extraverts. The over-conditioned introvert is a conformist, sticking to the rules, while the extravert takes risks and tends not to heed the consequences – he or she has not been socially so conditioned.

Eysenck points to the reactivity of the autonomic nervous system (ANS) as the biological basis of the neuroticism dimension (though in fact he traces it back still further to differences in the limbic system). The ANS is certainly highly active in emotion and produces the physical changes we associate with strong emotional reactions – sweating, paling of the skin, increased heart and respiration rates, and so on. There are considerable individual differences in autonomic reactivity, that is in the speed and strength of the ANS reaction to stress. Some people respond rapidly and strongly (high neuroticism in Eysenck's terms) while others do not. Again, whichever tendency the individual shows biologically may be enhanced or suppressed to an extent by subsequent learning experiences. Turning to the psychoticism dimension, the physiological rationale for this is much less clearly described, Eysenck's main thrust being to establish the viability of the concept rather than to explicate it in all respects. Although he has suggested (Eysenck, 1980) that the levels of androgen and other hormones may have significance for the psychoticism variable, much of the time he has been content to let others theorize about its biological basis.

In evolving his theory, Eysenck has developed a series of questionnaire measures of his dimensions. The two most recent are the Eysenck Personality Inventory (EPI) and the Eysenck Personality Questionnaire (EPQ), both of which incorporate extraversion and neuroticism scales, with the EPQ also containing a psychoticism scale. These are essentially research questionnaires and are not intended for use in making diagnostic or other

51

decisions about individual cases. As research questionnaires, they are acceptable in terms of reliability and validity (see pp. 85–8), though there are some reservations about the psychoticism scale; Eysenck admits that this is psychometrically inferior to the other two, and it has been suggested (Claridge and Chappa, 1973) that different development versions of the psychoticism scale seem to be measuring rather different concepts of psychoticism. One other point about his questionnaire measures needs making, and that is that a high score on the neuroticism (N) or psychoticism (P) scales does not necessarily mean that the person concerned is neurotic or psychotic. The implication of such scores, says Eysenck, is that under a high degree of stress the person with a high N score would tend to manifest a neurotic type of disorder while the person high in P would be likely to show a psychotic reaction (to get away from the potentially alarming misinterpretation of the psychoticism scale he suggests using the alternative term 'tough-mindedness').

Application and evaluation

So, according to this theory, extraversion, neuroticism and psychoticism (along with intelligence) can be identified as the main personality dimensions. By plotting an individual's score on measures of these three, Eysenck is able to predict a variety of things. For example, he predicts that the person who is high on neuroticism and high on extraversion will, if placed under stress, be likely to develop a neurotic hysterical reaction; a person high on neuroticism and high on introversion would be more likely to suffer an anxiety state (or obsessional state) under such circumstances; a combination of high psychoticism and low extraversion is indicative of a schizophrenic behavioural reaction.

Eysenck further suggests that neurotic problems are brought about by conditioning experiences of the individual and can thus be eliminated in the same way, through behaviour therapy (a term he is credited with originating). Other treatment approaches, particularly psychoanalysis, he attributes little or no value to. Going beyond the field of mental health, the theory has been applied to a diversity of social problems. In the realm of education, Eysenck has made out a case for streaming children by personality on the grounds that differences in arousal levels and conditionability are powerful influences on the learning process and need to be taken into account at least as much as differences in intelligence. He has had something to say about extrasensory perception, astrology, political beliefs, sexual behaviour, criminality, smoking and innumerable other topics. Eysenck might justifiably be said to have refreshed those parts that other psychologists seldom reach. Irrespective of whether his views are correct or not, almost every problem to which he has addressed himself has benefited from the debate his attention invariably stimulates.

Eysenck's theory is quite elegant and on first reading makes sense to a lot of people. Does the *evidence* support it, though? Studies of differences in conditionability between extraverts and introverts have been equivocal – some of them have certainly not found such differences (Eysenck, 1965). Eysenck has tended to criticize these investigations for not having followed appropriate methodology, for example the intensity of the stimuli used. But then one must ask, if this crucial difference in conditionability is such a delicate phenomenon as to be easily erased by quite small changes in experimental procedures, how can it possibly be responsible for all the gross differences in behaviour between introverts and extraverts we observe in everyday life? The conditioning experiences of the 'real' world outside the laboratory are not so carefully controlled as Eysenck's theory seems to require. And there are other problems. The evidence on arousal differences (due to the RAS differences) between introverts and extraverts has not always supported the theory as clearly as might be wished (Revelle *et al.*, 1980). Measures of introversion and neuroticism on Eysenck's questionnaires, supposedly quite independent, are frequently found to correlate, and the personality patterns predicted for various groups of psychiatric patients (as described above) are not uniformly supported, particularly in the case of hysterics (e.g. Ingham *et al.*, 1961). Finally, his concept of psychoticism has come in for sustained attack (Bishop, 1977; Block, 1978).

A theory with the precision, detail and breadth of Eysenck's is always going to be found wanting in our present state of knowledge. It has generated a vast amount of research and provided an invaluable model for personality investigations and will continue to do so for many years. Whilst the theory as it now stands is not adequate, some aspects of it, maybe even most, may well survive the test of time.

Cattell's theory

There are some broad similarities between R.B Cattell and H.J. Eysenck. Both received their training in psychology in Britain, both worked as applied psychologists (the former in the educational field and the latter in clinical practice) before concentrating on research, and both were influenced by the work of Spearman and Burt and have based their theories on the technique of factor analysis. Cattell's research on personality commenced after his move to the USA in the late 1930s. The first stage was to identify all trait names in the English language and, having removed synonyms, to rate a group of subjects on them. The resulting data were factor-analysed and fifteen factors emerged. Cattell then drew up a host of questionnaire items and administered them to subjects, the ensuing factor analysis throwing up 12 of the L factors (as Cattell calls factors based on ratings) discovered previously, plus 4 new ones – a total of 16 in all. These 16 factors, described in table 3, are measured by the widely used Cattell 16 PF (Personality Factor) Questionnaire. The last 4 factors are obtained *only* through questionnaire data and are thus designated Q factors; the remainder are found using ratings and questionnaires and are thus both L and Q factors.

Cattell based his approach on first-order factor analysis, unlike Eysenck, in this respect, who utilized second-order analysis. The difference between them mirrors the difference in thinking found between early British and American factor-analytic theories on the structure of intelligence (e.g. between Vernon and Burt, on the one hand, and Thurstone, on the other). The sixteen first-order factors are, according to Cattell, 'source traits' and are more important and useful in understanding behaviour than are second-order factors, which he considers too broad. There is, however, some correlation between the source traits, a feature that would be unacceptable to some factor theorists. Cattell argues that overlapping factors should to some extent be expected; for instance, well-integrated people are likely to be intelligent, hence a correlation between factors C and B (ego strength and intelligence).

The correlation of the first-order factors allows a number of second-order factors, or 'surface traits' as Cattell calls them, to be obtained. The first two, exvia and anxiety, seem to be the equivalent of Eysenck's extraversion and neuroticism dimensions (in fact, measures of Cattell's exvia and Eysenck's extraversion correlate around $+0.7$). Figure 3 illustrates the relationship of the

Table 3 Factors measured by the 16 Personality Factor Questionnaire.

Factor	Description of person with a low score	Description of person with a high score
A	RESERVED, cool, detached, aloof.	WARMHEARTED, easygoing, participating, outgoing.
B	CONCRETE THINKER, practically minded.	ABSTRACT THINKER, intellectual interests.
C	AFFECTED BY FEELINGS, emotionally less stable, easily upset.	EMOTIONALLY STABLE, faces reality, calm, mature.
E	SUBMISSIVE, mild, accommodating.	ASSERTIVE, dominant, aggressive, competitive.
F	SOBER, prudent, serious, taciturn.	HAPPY-GO-LUCKY, impulsively lively, enthusiastic.
G	EXPEDIENT, disregards rules, feels few obligations.	CONSCIENTIOUS, persevering, moralistic, straight-laced.
H	SHY, restrained, timid, threat-sensitive.	VENTURESOME, socially bold, uninhibited, spontaneous.
I	TOUGH-MINDED, self-reliant, realistic, no-nonsense.	TENDER-MINDED, gentle, over protected, sensitive.
L	TRUSTING, adaptable, free of jealousy, easy to get along with.	SUSPICIOUS, self-opinionated, hard to fool.
M	PRACTICAL, careful, conventional, regulated by external realities.	IMAGINATIVE, wrapped up in inner urgencies, careless of practical matters, bohemian.
N	FORTHRIGHT, natural, artless, unpretentious.	SHREWD, calculating, worldly, penetrating.
O	SELF-ASSURED, confident, complacent.	APPREHENSIVE, self-reproaching, worrying, troubled.
Q_1	CONSERVATIVE, respecting established ideas, tolerant of traditional difficulties.	EXPERIMENTING, liberal, analytical, free-thinking.
Q_2	GROUP-DEPENDENT, a 'joiner' and good follower.	SELF-SUFFICIENT, prefers own decisions, resourceful.
Q_3	UNDISCIPLINED SELF-CONFLICT, follows own urges, careless of social rules.	CONTROLLED, socially precise, compulsive, following self-image.
Q_4	RELAXED, tranquil, composed.	TENSE, frustrated, driven, overwrought.

second-order factors to their underlying source traits. By now, the reader will have been struck by the unusual nature of some of Cattell's trait names. The chief reasons behind the coining of such terms are that the source traits are usually broader concepts than the nearest word in common use would suggest and that the more popularly used terms are often insufficiently precise in meaning.

The results of his earlier work are enshrined in the 16PF Questionnaire, but Cattel's investigations go far beyond that. He has attempted to devise a battery of objective, behavioural tests of personality – the Objective-Analytic (O-A) battery – consisting of measures like galvanic skin response, reaction time and body-sway suggestibility. The information yielded by such tests Cattell calls T data. The factor analysis of such data has yielded no less than 21 factors (the O-A battery actually measures just 12 of these), some of which – but alas, only some – correspond to a number of second-order factors obtained from Q data. But the notion of taking behavioural measures, with their freedom from the distortion of response sets associated with questionnaire measures (see pp. 96–7), is a good one, even though difficult to put into effect.

Returning to the questionnaire data, when these are used with psychiatric patients, a series of twelve factors can be obtained that discriminate psychotics as a group. These include such traits as hypochondriasis, anxious depression and paranoia. Normal subjects score very low in these. Doing a second-order factor analysis

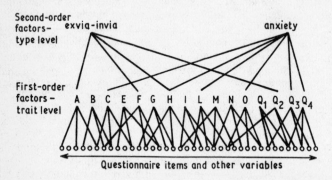

Figure 3 The hierarchical organization of factors derived from questionnaires. Surface traits, or second-order factors, are derived from underlying source traits, or first-order factors. (After Cattell, 1965, p. 118)

with abnormal subjects produces three factors, one of which resembles Eysenck's psychoticism factor. Cattell, however, differs from Eysenck in that he sees the likelihood of a fundamental discontinuity between normal personality and some types of severe disorder such as schizophrenia. Taking his recent work into account, Cattell now claims to be able, with L and Q data, to identify a total of 23 primary or source traits (though the 16 mentioned earlier are still the best established) and 8 second-order factors or surface traits in normal subjects, plus the 12 source and 3 surface traits associated with abnormal subjects (Cattell and Kline, 1977).

Thus far we have described Cattell's work on temperament, but he also has a lot to say about mood states, motivation and situations as they influence behaviour. Defining personality as 'what determines behaviour in a defined situation and a defined mood' (Cattell, 1965), he builds into the theory a greater recognition than does Eysenck of the transient fluctuations of behaviour in response to circumstances. Cattell's approach to these other variables is consistent with his work on traits. For example, he has developed the Eight State Questionnaire to measure the eight mood and state factors (depression, arousal, anxiety, fatigue, and so on) that have been discovered. These are not enduring characteristics of the individual but short-term phenomena, as when a normally calm individual shows considerable anxiety shortly after being involved in a car crash; any judgement of his personality that failed to take account of his mood state and its relation to the situation might well be mistaken. When discussing motivational aspects of personality, Cattell distinguishes between two sets of factors, *ergs*, which are biological drives (the ten main ones found to date include parental, mating, narcissism and acquisitiveness), and *sentiments*, which are culturally aquired drives (the six main sentiments include the self-sentiment, superego, religious and professional). Five of each type of motive are measured by the Motivation Analysis Test (MAT), which presents the subject with a series of objective tests in contrast to the normal questionnaire measures of motivation, which tend to ask the respondents whether they like or dislike certain activities and draw conclusions accordingly. Cattell is justifiably critical of the latter approach. He prefers to use indirect tests, as in the MAT, which supposedly reveal interests and drives through their effects on memory, mis-perception, speed of decision, and so on.

The scale of Cattell's attempt to specify and measure the main dimensions of personality, state and motivation is nothing if not ambitious. Only the crudest outline has been possible here, for there is a theoretical framework beyond his factor-analytic studies that is both comprehensive and speculative. One feature of Cattell's work promoting its application has been his propensity for producing psychological tests relevant to his theory. They range from the 16PF used with adults down to the Pre-School Personality Quiz for children in the 4–6 years range. For use in psychiatric settings, the Clinical Analysis Questionnaire has been developed. His work on intelligence has led to the construction of a culture-fair test of intelligence which sought to give a measure uncontaminated by ethnic and cultural background, but this particular venture does not seem to have been very successful.

Cattell has applied his ideas in almost as many fields as Eysenck and has not been afraid to generalize them to the functioning of society as a whole. In his book *New Morality from Science: Beyondism* (1975), he makes a number of proposals based on the scientific study of personality and relationships, including the suggestion that politicians should be psychologically selected. (The reader might like to muse on what qualities a politician should or should not have and what tests might be used in the selection battery. Would a lie-detector be a useful input to the process? Should we expect the same qualities in members of different parties?!) In a more limited sphere, the 16PF Questionnaire has been used in clinical work – mostly for research, as its validity is not adequate for making individual diagnoses (Williams *et al.*, 1972) – and in occupational selection and assessment. Cattell provided profiles of personality scores obtained for various diagnostic and occupational groups. To take an example of the latter, accountants show a profile that is marked by such features as low E, F and I and high B factor scores, indicating mild, sober, tough-minded and self-reliant individuals who are more intelligent than average (Cattell *et al.*, 1970), perhaps in line with the popular stereotype of accountants. Such profiles can be used in vocational counselling.

In the final analysis, Cattell's theory rests upon the factor-analytic method. It is therefore alarming to find that a number of studies using this method have not reproduced Cattell's source traits (e.g. Eysenck and Eysenck, 1969; Vagg and Hammond,

1976; Saville and Blinkhorn, 1976; Browne and Howarth, 1977), though there is a good level of agreement on the surface traits, in particular extraversion and anxiety. It can of course be argued, as Kline (1981b) does, that many of these failures to produce similar factor structures lie in the fact that different researchers have used different, and in some cases allegedly technically inadequate, factorial techniques. But the question then arises of how much faith can one place in a supposedly comprehensive and fundamental picture of personality that is so exquisitely dependent on a particular type of statistical analysis being performed in a particular way? This factorial structure of personality may be elegant, but it does not appear to be very robust. Not only do different statistical methods produce variations in the factors found, but so too do the type of data (L, Q or T) used.

Kelly's theory

George Kelly's Personal Construct Theory is quite unlike the theories mentioned so far. It is essentially an idiographic and phenomenological approach to personality. That is it emphasizes the uniqueness of each individual and seeks to understand the person by looking at his or her experience of the world and way of seeing it. The model for Kelly's theory is 'the personal scientist'. He argues that everyone has 'theories' (ideas, views, etc.) about their world – though somewhat lacking in organization and sophistication, perhaps – and that they form 'hypotheses' (expectations) on the basis of these. The hypotheses are tested in 'experiments' (behavioural interactions with other people and the environment), and are retained, modified or rejected in light of the results. So Kelly is saying that behaviour is basically anticipatory rather than reactive. The way we anticipate or predict the future is by developing a whole system of constructs, which are bipolar categorizations of similarities and differences perceived in the environment, e.g. loving–unloving, open-minded–dogmatic. Kelly suggests that our construct system is organized in a complex hierarchical network, with some broad constructs subsuming others. Thus the construct 'good–bad' might subsume the construct 'warm–cold' because the person feels that good people are, amongst other things, warm.

The constructs are our working hypotheses, to carry the scientist analogy further. If you construe somebody as being introverted, you might in effect be hypothesizing or predicting that he or she will not want to go to a noisy party with you. You might test this hypothesis out by asking the individual, and depending on the outcome you would confirm or disconfirm your prediction. It follows from this that a person's construct system, this framework of dimensions used for understanding the world, is not a static thing. It should be constantly evolving and changing. Kelly describes various types of change that take place within the construct system. An example of this would be the tightening or loosening of construing. One might move from tighter, more precisely defined constructs when dealing with clear-cut subjects (as when construing physical objects) to looser, vaguer constructs when dealing with more complex and less well-understood subjects (such as other people).

The theory, then, tries to describe individuals in terms of their construct systems, how they are organized and how they change. All the phenomena of motivation and emotion are interpreted in this way; thus, 'threat' is the awareness of an imminent comprehensive change in one's most central (core) constructs, and anxiety is the awareness that what you are confronted with is not within the framework of your existing construct system – you do not know how to construe it. The material we are dealing with is exclusively how a person conceptualizes events, things and people. Kelly stated his theory in a fairly abstract form to avoid the limitations of the time and culture in which it was evolved. He also stated it in its entirety, a comprehensive and elaborate theory that has few rivals in psychology. As Bannister and Fransella (1971) say, it would be a brave and foolish individual who claimed to know what learning 'theory' or Freudian 'theory' were – they are too loosely formulated and poorly integrated to justify the term 'theory'.

Personal Construct Theory is not easy to grasp on first acquaintance, but it does perhaps become more comprehensible when one looks at the assessment device (not a test as such) that Kelly devised on the basis of it. This is the repertory grid, one of the most widely used psychological investigative techniques of recent years. In its basic form, it goes something like this: a person is asked to name the most important figures in his or her life – father, mother, spouse, boss, best friend, etc. – and is then presented with three of these, the names being written on separate cards, and asked, 'In what way are two of these alike and different from the third?' The person might say, 'Well, my father and my boss are both assertive and my best friend of the opposite sex is fairly docile.' That – assertive–docile – is the first construct, and would then be applied to all the remaining figures, each being assigned to one or other pole of the construct. Next, another triad of figures would be presented and the whole process repeated. This goes on until the individual has produced either all the constructs he or she can (seldom more than twenty-five with one set of stimulus figures) or all that are necessary for the purpose in hand. By arranging all the names of the people construed – known as the *elements* – along the top of a piece of paper and the constructs down the side, you end up with a grid (hence the name). The grid shows on which end of each construct each element is placed, using a simple binary system of ticks and crosses (see figure 4).

Various forms of analysis, ranging from very simple methods through to factor analysis can be applied to the grid. Often they will show that many of the constructs overlap to the extent that they mean much the same thing, and analysis throws up the fact that most people are really only using 3 to 6 main constructs. Grid data not only show what those main constructs are, but how important people are seen on them. Sometimes, the individual is not aware of the relationship that, for example, he is seeing between his girl friend and his mother. (See Shaw and McKnight, 1981, for a readable account of the repertory grid technique.)

Elements

Constructs	A	B	C	D	E	etc.
1	✓	✓	✗	✗	✓	
2	✗	✓	✗	✓	✓	
3	✗	✗	✗	✓	✗	
4	✓	✓	✗	✗	✓	
etc.						

Figure 4 The repertory grid.

There are many different ways of using the repertory grid, which has proved to be very flexible. It has the great virtue of allowing people to say how they see things, rather than being forced on to the dimensions supplied by the psychologist. Though grids can be used nomothetically with supplied constructs, this is moving a long way from Kelly's original idea. The elements used do not have to be people. They could be jobs, consumer products, characters in a play, buildings and almost anything else. Amongst other things, the grid has been used in studying the changing mutual perceptions of people in group therapy, in looking at how people view different kinds of car, and in examining the contrasting ways effective and ineffective salesmen view their clients. As a technique, the repertory grid can stand on its own – one does not have to espouse the underlying theory to accept its usefulness. The theory of personal constructs has generated a good deal of research, mainly thanks to the availability of the grid to test out its predictions (for a review of the research, see Adams-Webber, 1979).

George Kelly has, along with Carl Rogers, put the 'ego' back into personality. By concentrating on the individual's conscious adjustment to the world and on the importance of trying to get to grips with a person's experience in order to understand him or her properly, Personal Construct Theory has been invaluable in reminding us that nobody reacts to a stimulus – people react to what they *interpret* that stimulus to be. The fact that the theory completely ignores genetic or physiological factors, and many other things besides, is perhaps forgivable in the light of that contribution.

Overview of personality theories

Even allowing for the fact that depth theories were touched on in chapter 2, there has only been space here to skim over the surface of personality theory. Nothing has been said of the works of Carl Rogers, Alfred Adler, Karen Horney and many others. However, this is not a text on personality as such (see Fonagy, 1984, in this series), and what we have done is to concentrate on those theories of personality (Eysenck's and Cattell's) that are most closely identified with the field of individual differences. Both are examples of the psychometric model of personality, resting on the use of factor analysis of psychological measures to identify basic traits. This approach has been with us for a good many years now, and not everyone is impressed by the sum of its achievements. Vernon, writing in 1964, concluded that the trait and factor approach just has not worked well enough. Despite generating a vast amount of research, he said, no one has managed to produce a battery of tests that most other psychologists have enough faith in to use for practical purposes. Since 1964, it would be true to say that the use of trait measures has grown and that some, like Cattell's 16PF Questionnaire, have won a fair degree of acceptance. Also, as we noted earlier, there is some element of agreement in the findings of Eysenck and Cattell. However, the doubts remain and have surfaced in the form of the situationalist critique that was described in the introductory section of this chapter.

Perhaps the important thing to remember is that traits are not *veridical*; that is they are not really 'there', running through personality like so many seams of coal running through rock. Like most other personality variables, traits are abstractions – they are inferred on the basis of behaviour. This being the case, there is no one 'right' way to look at personality, no one 'correct' perspective. There may be some approaches which are generally more useful than others, or within any particular kind of theory there may be some variety which seems to predict behaviour better than others. But we are unlikely to end up with one 'approved' theory in the foreseeable future. Even when our knowledge has advanced significantly, we will probably still find it useful to take different perspectives on the individual's personality according to what we need to know and why. Thus, some disagreement amongst the trait theorists should not be seen as disproving the value of this particular model of personality.

Criticisms of the psychometric model apart, how should theories of personality be evaluated more generally? Some of the criteria that might be used are implicit or explicit in what has already been said. The main ones are:

1 How complete is the theory in its explanation of human personality in all its ramifications? Does it take everything into account – the individual's self-concept, the role of the unconscious, the influence of heredity and physiological factors, and so on? Personality theories have been characterized by their comprehensive nature. They are far broader in their scope than most other fields of psychology, where the norm is to develop theories that deal with specific psychological functions (like memory) or with a limited range of psychological reactions (as

in abnormal and social psychological theories). Not all personality theories seek to be comprehensive, of course. Some quite openly disregard some concepts or levels of analysis that they consider mistaken or irrelevant. None the less, this is a worthwhile and informative criterion against which to view such theories.

2 The theory should be internally consistent and logical in its formulation. One should be able to deduce things from it, and these deductions should be testable and thus open to disconfirmation.

3 The theory should be supported by empirical investigation; it should have the weight of experimental evidence to back up its assertions.

4 To what extent is the theory supported by another kind of evidence – its usefulness in applied settings? Again, this is a typical feature of personality theories. Many of them have their roots in observations and data collected in real-life settings of hospitals, companies, consulting rooms, and the like, rather than in the laboratory. But just how useful does each theory prove to be in terms of, say, understanding what sort of relationships an individual will form as part of a management group, or predicting such things as career choice or predisposition to psychological breakdown? Sometimes these questions can be answered empirically, sometimes we are relying on the judgement of the applied psychologist or whoever it is using the theory, with all the implications of the subjectivity of that judgement.

5 How far does a theory advance our knowledge? A theory that yields many hypotheses and a lot of research might be judged as having contributed more to the field than one that generates less in these respects.

The reader might like to compare the theories of Freud, Eysenck and Kelly according to these criteria (excepting perhaps (4) above, though you might ask yourself whether you feel each theory is useful in giving *you* insights into your own behaviour).

'Narrow-band' theories

Up to now we have considered only major theories of personality; theories that try, each in their own way, to explain a wide range of behaviours. However, much of the research in this field does not relate to such theories or anything like them. Instead it focuses on more limited concepts that might be useful in understanding individual differences. Following the example of Peck and Whitlow (1975), we might describe these as 'narrow-band' theories, though few if any of them are truly worthy of the term 'theory'. It is not possible to mention more than a small number of them here, but they will serve as examples of an important and burgeoning aspect of personality study.

Self-esteem

Many aspects of the individual's perception of himself or herself have attracted the attention of personality researchers, but the concept of self-esteem has been probably the most studied in this area. It refers to a person's judgement of self-worth, which arises partly from the feedback obtained on the effectiveness of behaviour from childhood onwards. Coopersmith (1967, 1968) in a study of young boys and their families found that the boys with high self-esteem tended to be those higher in competence, better thought of by their parents and with parents also possessing high self-esteem.

There are numerous (mostly questionnaire) measure of self-esteem and they have consistently been shown to relate to important aspects of behaviour. For example, high self-esteem is associated with higher levels of aspiration and less willingness to conform to situational influence. It is also found to correlate positively with job-performance indices (Korman, 1976). Very low levels of self-esteem are characteristic of people suffering from depression, though whether poor self-esteem is a predisposing factor in depression or a result of the disorder is not entirely clear. One theory suggests that there are individual differences in the way people explain their successes and failures. Some individuals persistently attribute their success to external factors such as luck or fate and their failures to internal factors like their own incompetence or unattractiveness; this kind of person tends to suffer from low self-esteem and to be susceptible to depression (Abramson *et al.*, 1978). People who always see success as stemming from their own abilities, and failure as always arising out of external factors – bad luck, other people, etc. – would probably have rather high self-esteem, though their confidence in themselves might have little objective basis.

Internal–external locus of control

This grew out of the social learning theory of behaviour (Rotter, 1954). The notion is that people's life history of reinforcement tends to create general beliefs and expectancies either that their behaviour is effective in obtaining desired ends or that events are pretty much out of their hands. Internal people have generally found that they can influence and control important sources of reinforcement and can see themselves as masters of their own fate. External people have perceived a lack of control of what happens to them and come to attribute events to sources outside themselves – luck, fate, powerful others. As this is a dimension, most people will be in between these extremes. The degree of internality or externality of the individual will have a range of behavioural consequences. Internals will be expected to be more dominant and effective across a wide range of activities, while externals would be more passive and less likely to attempt coping behaviours. Not surprisingly, there is plenty of evidence to show that underprivileged and minority groups tend to be highly external. Once again, there is something of a problem in measurement. The Rotter (1966) I–E Scale used in many studies has been shown as assessing a number of different aspects of control, for example some people may be internal as far as they view their immediate circumstances but quite external in their perception of how much influence they have on society and social institutions. More refined scales have thus had to be developed (Lefcourt, 1982).

Machiavellianism

The idea behind this goes back 400 years to the Italian philosopher, Niccolò Machiavelli. In his book *The Prince*, he gave detailed suggestions of how to manipulate others in the pursuit of power. Rather more recently, Christie and Geis (1970) developed a questionnaire measure of Machiavellian tendencies, the Mach scale. People who score highly on it have a propensity for ruthless, self-centred strategies in interpersonal relationships; such people trust no one, are very willing to lie and are apt to believe that it is best to tell people what they want to hear. Large-scale use of the test confirms what your experience probably tells you, there is no shortage of high-Mach individuals around. In fact they can even be identified amongst 10-year-olds (Kraut and Paice, 1976). High-Mach people maintain cool detachment in their dealings with others and work pragmatically towards their goals. They are socially skilled in influencing others. When they tell lies, they are seen as being more truthful than are low-Mach-scorers when they are lying (Geis and Moon, 1981). And further evidence of their effectiveness in social transactions is provided by Christie and Geis (1970), in a study where groups of three subjects were given money and told that it would be split between any two of them who could agree on how to divide it, the third person getting nothing. Faced with such a situation, high-Mach subjects tended to end up with a far greater share of the money than did low-Mach subjects.

Repression-sensitization

Freud believed that the ego's main defence against open expression of the id's instincts was repression, a mechanism for keeping things out of consciousness. Sometimes this does not work very well, and the individual experiences anxiety – a warning signal that id material is close to breaking into consciousness. In this case, further repression is often required. So for Freud, the basic defence was repression, a way of preventing threatening material from entering or re-entering consciousness. Later experimental work, however, showed that while some people characteristically deal with threat by repressing it, others adopt a quite different strategy. They prefer a sensitizing, vigilant strategy that allows them to identify sources of stress and make preparatory coping responses to help alleviate them. A measure of these tendencies, the Repression-Sensitization Scale, was developed by Byrne *et al.* (1963). People identified as repressors on the scale tend to see emotional reactions as bad and deny them, while sensitizers regard them as positive indicators of honesty and sensitivity. As one might expect from this, sensitizers are more likely to seek psychotherapy than are repressors (Thelen, 1969). Interestingly, when placed in stressful situations repressors show a higher level of physiological reaction than do sensitizers, but verbally describe themselves as *less* anxious than the latter (Scarpetti, 1973). In some ways, this fits in quite nicely with Freud's ideas on repression.

Type A personality

This is a more limited concept than some of the others we have mentioned, dealing as it does with a particular behaviour pattern and its consequences. But those consequences are literally a matter of life and death. Type A, or coronary-prone, behaviour is marked by extreme competitiveness, aggression, impatience, quickness of speech and movement, and haste. It has been described as 'hurry-sickness'. Type A people seem to be trying to control all aspects of their lives, even potentially uncontrollable ones. Friedman and Rosenman (1974) proposed a link between this behaviour pattern and coronary heart disease, and a large amount of evidence has proved them right (Jenkins, 1976). For example, Friedman and his colleagues studied 3000 initially healthy men between the ages of 39 and 59. They were classified into Type A or Type B (simply absence of Type A behaviours) and followed up after two and a half years. In the 39–49 age range Type A men had 6.5 times the incidence of coronary disease found in the Type B individuals; the corresponding figure for the 50–59 age group was 1.9 times the incidence. Research is quite conclusive that these and similar findings are not accountable for in terms of differences in diet, exercise or smoking.

There are many other personality constructs that could have been described had space permitted. The ones that have been covered show the value of these more limited approaches to understanding personality. The next chapter deals with an area of individual differences that in many respects overlaps with personality theories, namely motivation.

6 Motivation

Chapters 3 and 4 were concerned with abilities, with the question 'What can I do?' Chapter 5 was concerned with personality, with the question 'What am I like?' or 'How do I generally behave?' This chapter concerns itself with motivational directions, with the question 'What do I want?' It is concerned not so much with possibilities opened up by abilities, but with choices between alternatives. It looks at the roads people choose to take and the decisions that are taken at forks along the road. It looks at how individuals differ in what interests them, in what they want from a job or their life, at what they want to achieve, what they desire, need or value. In a word, it is concerned with what motivates them. We will be concerned, though, only with those areas where we are conscious of our motives and where they can be measured objectively. Unconscious motivation may well be important in explaining some parts of behaviour and has been touched on in the section on Freud (chapter 2). But this book is mostly concerned with psychometrics rather than with psychodynamics or psychoanalytic approaches and the projective techniques associated with them.

Interests

Interests, like values, motives and attitudes, are an important aspect of a person's personality, broadly defined. However, the concepts of interests, values and attitudes overlap so that it is difficult to establish the crucial differences between them. Instruments used to measure, say, interests have items which could be interpreted as reflecting values or attitudes. To say that someone is interested in religious affairs, or in taking Holy Orders, says much about their values and their attitudes towards other aspects of their life.

Measurement of interests

The measurement of interests has a long history in psychology, and started with the objective of improving occupational guidance. When someone is trying to choose a job or career, knowledge of interests as well as abilities and values should be important components of the decision. The aim was to help individuals identify their interests so as to improve the match between those interests and the requirements, opportunities and satisfactions of jobs. Sophisticated measuring instruments have been developed, just as they have for personality and intelligence. You may feel that it is less necessary to develop these measures in the field of interests than in other areas. After all, why can we not just ask someone what types of work or educational courses interest him or her? One problem with this is that some people have very little idea of what they are interested in. Secondly, most people, especially young people, have only a limited knowledge of different jobs or courses. They do not know what aspects of those courses or jobs might coincide with their interests. Moreover, many jobs, such as those of car worker, barmaid, window cleaner, barrister or accountant, have strong stereotypes attached to them (see Shackleton, 1980, for example). The reality of the job is often different from its popular image.

So, less direct questioning methods have been evolved, using tests. Test items are chosen based on aspects of everyday life such as people, objects or actions about which individuals can express interest or lack of interest. Responses are then 'empirically keyed' (or criterion-keyed – see chapter 7), meaning that people at present employed in different occupations are asked to say how far these different aspects of life interest them. People in certain occupations have been found to have reasonably good agreement on what they are interested or not interested in and there are consistent differences in these interests between occupations. So, it is possible to ask someone about matters not necessarily related to jobs, such as his or her reading habits or school subjects preferred and see how far these interests are the same as the interests of people who are successful in different jobs. The testee can then be advised on his or her choice of occupation with the empirical knowledge of occupational interests in mind. The 'blind empiricism' of the criterion-keying method, though, means that the tests have little theoretical interest. In fact, the whole field of interests is not a well-developed one theoretically.

Reliability and validity of interests

The Strong Vocational Interest Blank (SVIB) is one such test developed by the criterion-keying method. The test has 400 items and takes about an hour to complete. It has a very satisfactory reliability and validity (see pp. 85–8 for a definition of these concepts). A study of 134 women psychologists (Campbell, 1971) showed that their pattern of interests hardly changed at all between 1942 and 1966. At each of these two test dates, the group scored highest on interests related to psychologists, next highest on those related to speech pathologists and physicians, and very low on those of interest to high-school teachers of physical education. This stability is despite considerable social changes during that time as well as changes in the role of women and in the job of psychologist. Adolescents are more likely to change interests than are adults and in both age groups a few individuals show large changes. Yet even from as early as adolescence, there is a remarkable consistency of interest pattern.

Predictive validity studies with samples over long intervals also show good agreement between the original occupational profile based on the test and the occupation eventually followed. Similarly, subjects who acted on the SVIB results were more satisfied in their jobs, stayed in the job longer and were more successful in terms of money and position that subjects who did not follow the SVIB advice. However, we must be careful not to run away with the idea that interest in an occupation leads to success. The relationship between the two is not a strong one and this is hardly surprising. Just because you are interested in an occupation does not mean that you will be successful in it. Abilities, work habits, grasped opportunities that come your way and many other factors have a hand in success. But it helps to be interested in the path you have chosen for yourself, and to have similar interests to those travelling the same path.

In 1974 the SVIB was considerably revised, and renamed the Strong–Campbell Interest Inventory (SCII). There are now 325 items which can only be scored by computer. The authors suggest that the research results from the SVIB apply to the SCII but in some respects this may be wishful thinking.

Criticisms of interest tests

British psychometricians, such as Kline (1976), tend to be unenthusiastic about the SVIB. For one thing, this American test is based on American norms. Jobs with the same title in different countries are often very different in practice and some job titles, like forest ranger, hardly translate at all. So it is highly questionable how far SVIB results apply in Britain. Secondly, it takes a long time to complete and score the test, time which might be spent much more usefully by both client and counsellor in vocational guidance. Finally and crucially, the test does not correlate with a job criterion any better than does the straightforward question of stated interest. So, if a subject can be specific about a job (often *not* the case), we are no better off from our time and trouble with the SVIB and other similar tests than if we just ask the client 'What are you interested in?'

Similar criticisms apply to other American tests, such as the well-known Kuder Interest Tests. Reliability and validity studies show that the scores on these are stable over time and predict occupational satisfaction and success, but again the tests are lengthy, are no better than a simple statement of interest in a job, and are based on American jobs which are often very different from British jobs even if they have the same job title. Moreover the Kuder, along with another well-known test, the Rothwell-Miller, asks subjects to *rank* jobs or interests, which brings a whole set of problems, as explained in the following quote:

> If subject A and subject B both choose outdoor interests first and mechanical interests second (which is perfectly possible and quite likely), this does not necessarily mean that their interests are similar. The glutton and the anorexic, for example,

could easily rank roast beef and curry in the same order. Nor does it mean that subjects A and B like outdoor things more than subject C who ranks them third. C may have a wide range of deep interests while A and B are apathetic adolescents interested only in sex and its concomitants. Thus, even though a counsellor may learn an individual's order of preference for certain interests from the *Kuder* test, this is not necessarily as useful as might otherwise be thought. To draw norms based on these individual preferences (as the *Kuder* does) for this test is obviously quite inappropriate. Therefore, it is rather difficult to support the use of the *Kuder* or similar tests either in practice or research. (Kline, 1976, p. 100)

The problem revolves around what are known as ipsative scores. When each preference or interest is expressed, not in absolute terms, but in relation to every other interest on the test, the resulting scores are called 'ipsative'. It is all right as long as we remember that the test scores relate to an individual and allow us to make comparisons of the relative strength of interests for that individual. The problem comes when we try to compare or combine one individual's score with others. As the Kline quote makes clear, two individuals with identical scores may differ considerably in the absolute strength of their interests which makes comparing individuals difficult. Combining individual, ipsative scores into norms is statistically inappropriate and the result confusing at best and meaningless at worst. The Kuder, the Strong and the Rothwell–Miller are all ipsative tests and fall foul of the statistical and interpreting problems.

A much more recent interest measure that is unusual in design and is not ipsative is the Brook Reaction Test. It comprises about 80 stimulus words which are read out to the subject at the rate of 1 every 12 seconds. Subjects write down the first word they think of, followed by the word that this reminds them of, and so on. Usually around 3 words are generated within the 12 seconds allowed. The test uses words which have more than one meaning so that the generated words can refer to a wide variety of responses. The generated words are then categorized by the tester according to 22 interest scales including business, food, intellectual, legal and military, and an interest-scale score is arrived at. As yet there is little research on the validity of the Brook Reaction Test but it opens up exciting new possibilities in the area of interest measurement.

Values

There has been an increasing interest in the concept of values, particularly values associated with work, over the past ten or fifteen years. Consequently there are a large number of measures of values available, which aim to assess the evaluative orientations of an individual, that is the sorts of behaviours, object or direction that he or she values. Examples of dominant values are economic, social, religious and political. Obviously people differ in the importance they attach to each of these values. As you can see, the concept of values, and therefore the instruments used to measure it, have much in common with the concepts and measures of interests, attitudes, needs and personality. This has led to a considerable problem of confused terminology in the literature. We must first try to disentangle the definition of values from those other, similar concepts.

Definitions

One can think of values, and attempt to distinguish them from similar concepts, in four main ways – as an evaluative concept, a non-differential concept, a hierarchical concept and a complementary concept. We will look at each briefly, but a more detailed account can be found in Pryor (1980) and Shackleton and Engel (1982).

In common usage as well as in the psychological literature, the term 'values' often has a strong *evaluative* component. Thus Rokeach (1973) sees values as the central part of the belief system about how an individual feels he or she ought to behave or about the value of some 'end-state of existence' that is personally or socially preferable. Others have argued with the '*ought* to behave' element of values, but agree that they are based on individual preferences.

Other writers adopt the rather unsatisfactory position of tolerating the *non-differentiation* of concepts. Thus Katzell (1964) accepts the range of labels – values, goals, needs, desires, interests – and lumps them together without trying to differentiate them. He is happy enough that they all generally indicate that a person perceives job features as 'attractive or repellent, desirable or undesirable'.

Many writers come to grips with the definitional problem by seeing the concepts as a *hierarchy*. For Rokeach (1973), the value system is a hierarchy of ideals so that an adult is seen as having tens of thousands of beliefs, thousands of attitudes but only dozens of values. Super (1973) also sees the relationship between needs, values and interests in a hierarchical model: 'Values are objectives that one seeks to attain to satisfy a need. Interests are the specific activities and objects through which values can be attained and needs met' (Super, 1973, p. 190). And so the hierarchy from top to bottom consists of needs, followed by values and then interests. Needs, such as the need for nourishment, shelter, love and achievement, are seen as fundamental requirements of the human being for his or her well-being. They are so fundamental, so removed from specific everyday actions, and so capable of being met in a variety of ways, that they cannot help us predict educational or occupational behaviour. Values and interests, on the other hand, are closer to everyday life and better predictors of behaviour.

Similar to the hierarchical model is the view that many of the concepts are dissimilar but *complementary*. Pryor (1978) sees both interests and values as preferences, distinguished by the category of things preferred: 'In the context of career development the relevant categories are activities (for interests) and qualities (for values) in one's work.' Thus interests can be seen as work-activity preferences and values as work-aspect preferences. Activities (interests) might be reading books, building furniture or programming computers, while work aspects (values) might be altruism, characterized by helping to build a better society or giving aid to those in need, or security, meaning work where you can be reasonably sure your job will last.

Measurement of values

A well-known and long-standing instrument is the Study of Values, developed by Allport, Vernon and Lindzey. This was designed to measure six basic values including theoretical (characterized by a dominant interest in the discovery of truth), economic (emphasizing useful and practical values) and political (placing value on personal power and influence not only limited to public politics). It is an ipsative test and so the authors caution against using percentiles or normative types of score. Its reliability and validity seem adequate. Retests after a month or two have shown reliabilities between 0.77 and 0.90. Regarding validity, different groups such as theological and medical students have shown results in the expected direction.

A measure more specifically focused on work values is the Work Values Inventory (WVI), designed by Super. It contains fifteen values such as security (work where job conditions are secure), achievement (work which gives one a feeling of accomplishment in doing a job well) and creativity (work in which one invents new things or develops new ideas). The WVI has been tested in a variety of forms and widely used in research since 1951. Super says that it can be used to understand the values of a client in educational or vocational counselling, of an applicant for employment or as an aid for a client to clarify his or her own values and the appropriateness of a particular training, education or employment. However, there is some doubt about its reliability. One study did report good retest reliability for the scale scores over a two-week interval, but another study by Gable and Pruzek (1971) showed that the internal consistency of some of the scales was suspect. Its use as a test is therefore somewhat in doubt.

Finally, a test developed in Australia by Pryor (1981) called the Work Aspects Preference Scale is promising. It has 13 values in a 52-item, 5-point rating-scale format. Good retest reliability and validity results are reported by Pryor and the scale may well prove useful in vocational guidance in the future.

Rokeach's studies

Rokeach (1973) is one investigator who has done a great deal of empirical work on values, based on large samples of people. He showed, for example, that Americans ranked the terminal values (meaning things to strive for) of 'a world at peace', 'family security' and 'freedom' highest, while 'an exciting life', 'pleasure' and 'a world of beauty' were lowest. Remember, though, that this ipsative measure *forces* some items lower than others, just by the ranking procedure. It does not mean that the sample was against a beautiful world! Sex differences were as we might have expected (especially at the time of the study, the late 1960s): men were more achievement-oriented and materialistic, women more in favour of peace, love and happiness.

Rokeach also examined the values of the supporters and advocates of different political orientations. He analysed the content of the writings of advocates of four ideologies – Lenin (communism), Hitler (fascism), Barry Goldwater (capitalism) and several socialists – by asking judges to count the frequency of values expressed in these writings. The socialists put freedom 1 and equality 2 in rank order of values. Hitler ranked freedom 16 and equality 17 out of 17 ranks. Lenin ranked equality 1 and freedom 17. Goldwater ranked freedom 1 and equality 16. Simply put:

	Freedom	*Equality*
Socialism	High	High
Capitalism	High	Low
Communism	Low	High
Fascism	Low	Low

Rokeach sees this as a general model of political ideology. Other evidence on the importance of values comes from many different subject groups, including prison inmates, who ranked 'honest' lower and 'wisdom' higher than did non-offenders, and regular church-goers, who ranked 'salvation' much higher than did those who did not attend regularly. In summary, Rokeach has shown that values do differentiate individuals and that the value differences are linked to behaviour in meaningful ways.

Criticism of values

There seems little doubt that values are an important element of individual differences. This is particularly so in the area of work values, where most of the research has been done. Zytowski (1970) in a review of research and theory on work values concluded that values may be *more* important than interests in planning and choosing careers. The process of choosing a career is probably a compromise between interests, abilities, values and opportunities.

There are two major difficulties, though, in whole-heartedly accepting the importance of values. One is that values have not been shown to be conceptually and empirically distinct from, but related to, interests. The research results are ambiguous. Super (1962) reported high correlations between the Allport–Vernon–Lindzey Study of Values and the Strong Vocational Interest Blank, while Ivey (1963) found that a Kuder interest scale did not correlate highly with the Work Values Inventory. A review by Thorndike *et al.* (1968) of a number of studies showed correlations lower than one would expect if interests and values are related.

The second difficulty is that the instruments devised to measure values have not been as well developed nor as extensively used in research as have interest measures. The two difficulties are related. If instruments had been devised and used then we might have a clearer view of the part played by values in individual differences and vocational choice, and how they empirically differ from interests. Yet how can good instruments be devised if we are not sure how values differ from other individual difference variables?

In conclusion, we still maintain that values are important. The research that has been done suggests that values are related to, but different from, interests, and consistent with a hierarchical or complementary model, and that a useful way of thinking of work values is as preferences for work qualities, while interests are preferences for work activities.

Need for achievement

Need for achievement can be seen as a narrow-band personality theory (see chapter 5), but is probably better described as a social motive, along with such others as need for power and need for approval. The first clear formulation of an achievement motive came from Murray in 1938, but the concept was developed by McClelland (1951) and it is with his name that need for achievement, or nAch as it is abbreviated, is normally associated. The nAch variable is concerned with the desire to compete against a standard and with the individual's emotional reactions in situations where they compete and where their performance can be evaluated. Work on the concept was extended by Atkinson (1957) who looked not just at the need to achieve but also at the other half of the picture, the fear of failure. The general theory is that people with high nAch approach tasks of intermediate difficulty, rather than tasks that are very easy or very difficult. Easy tasks provide no challenge; competing against such an easy standard is not motivating; achieving easy tasks gives no sense of accomplishment. Very difficult tasks do provide lots of challenge but also do not motivate the high nAch person since success is so unlikely. Those low on nAch also go for intermediate-difficulty tasks but are much less positive in their tendency to approach them. Those with high fear of failure (FF) opt for either very easy tasks – with a high chance of success – or very hard tasks, where the difficulty can be used as an excuse for not being successful. The evidence supporting these predictions is quite good.

However, one of the main problems plaguing the nAch field is the method of measurement. Some investigators, like McClelland, treat nAch as an unconscious personality characteristic and use the Thematic Apperception Test (TAT), a projective instrument. This consists of a series of cards showing pictures of people in varying situations, although it is not clear what they are doing. Respondents are asked to create stories around the activities shown on the cards, particularly about what has happened, what is happening and what will happen. There is a complicated scoring scheme, developed by Atkinson (1957), which is used to score the stories for achievement actions and images. For example if someone creates a story around the central character studying hard to improve an examination performance, competing against other clever people in order to further their career, he or she would get a high nAch score. The trouble is that the TAT scores are not often closely correlated with other measures of achievement such as examination results. Of course, many things apart from just nAch affect examination scores, such as luck, ability, interest in the subject and parental pressure, among a host of factors. So perhaps the low correlation is not very surprising. However, few strong correlations between TAT nAch scores and other achievement behaviour have been reported.

Other investigators regard nAch as a conscious social need and use self-report questionnaires (Fineman, 1977). The validity evidence here is also somewhat equivocal, although some studies using such questionnaires have shown that entrepreneurs (who we would expect to be highly achievement-orientated) do have higher nAch scores than similar businessmen working in large firms. Similarly, successful businessmen in a number of different cultures have higher nAch scores than do their less successful compatriots.

Another so far unresolved issue is the question of how stable nAch scores are over time, particularly when measured with the TAT. The scores suggest that it is not a very stable disposition, though we might expect it to be. In other words, the test–retest reliability of the TAT is rather low. A number of reasons for, and defences of, the low test–retest reliability have been made (see Weiner, 1980, for a summary) but it casts doubt on the usefulness of the TAT as a nAch measure. Also there is the question of how it comes about that one person with a high nAch directs that need into business activities, while another concentrates on competing in sport and another strives for academic excellence. The more general issue of how high nAch comes about has been researched and seems to be related to child-rearing practices, particularly the emphasis on independence training early in childhood development (Winterbottom, 1958), but the question of the *direction* of the need and its generalization to different spheres of achievement is far from being answered.

To conclude, the idea that individuals differ in their need to achieve has prompted a great deal of research, and no doubt will continue to do so. Despite measurement difficulties, we have accumulated a number of findings about nAch. It looks as if it is related to the difficulty of tasks we set ourselves, to success in the business world and to child-rearing practices. It may even be related to the economic success of countries. Protestantism and early independence training seem to produce societies with more people with higher nAch, which leads to economic development. Successful attempts have been made, particularly in developing countries, to train people in need for achievement.

Finally, research has been directed at sex differences and nAch, and at the possibility that females have a motive to avoid success or a 'fear of success' (Horner, 1972). While later research has thrown considerable doubt on this idea, it is well established that females generally have a lower expectancy of success than males, and that female success is often perceived to result from effort and luck, rather than from ability. We can expect to find out much more about need for achievement in the coming years.

Need for power

Like achievement, the power motive is and has been a driving force of many societies and individuals. From the individualistic lust for sexual conquests of Don Juan to the quest for power and domination of many an imperialistic nation or war-lord, power has motivated and fascinated people. Not surprisingly, therefore, psychologists have turned their attention to describing and measuring it. They have been interested in many aspects of individual differences and power, including the extent to which we feel powerful or in control of events (measured by internal–external locus of control questionnaires) and beliefs about how and over whom power should be exercised in order to beat or win over other people (such as the Machiavellianism personality questionnaire), both of which were touched upon in chapter 5, as well as in the quest for power or the power motive, described here. The need for power can be defined as the desire to control or influence others, and to be recognized as powerful. As need for achievement (nAch), so also need for power (nPower) has been measured by the TAT.

Research has shown that people in leadership positions, where power can be exercised, do have higher nPower scores than others. Thus Winter (1973) found that officers in American university student organizations scored higher than non-officers. Other students high in nPower became members of staff–student committees and workers on the university radio station and newspaper – all positions where power can be exercised in western universities. Winter also showed that students high in nPower behaved in ways which helped them achieve positions of power. These strategies included being visible, such as writing to the university newspaper; developing a loyal network of associates who were not themselves visible or known; and not being afraid of being unpopular.

The power motive is also related to career choice. Studies have shown that male graduates in British and American universities who are high in nPower choose careers that involve direct, interpersonal power, such as business, teaching, psychology, journalism and the church. Note that each of these professions allows the person to have immediate and personal power to direct and control the behaviour of other people, often with the use of rewards and punishments. Other careers, such as in science, law and even politics, do not permit such direct, legitimate and interpersonal power to be exercised. They are more indirectly and abstractly associated with power and are not so likely to be pursued by men with high nPower scores.

An interesting aspect of nPower, and one which has been investigated, is its relationship to prestige and displays of power symbols. Prestigious possessions can be seen as one of the ways that power is legitimately expressed in our society. The studies of students by Winter (1973) have shown that nPower is related to having prestige articles such as a tape recorder, television set and framed pictures, despite there being no correlation between nPower and spending money. Among businessmen, nPower is associated with the number of credit cards they regularly carry. You may have noticed how advertisements for one particular credit card encourage the view that only the rich and powerful are worthy enough to carry it, and that possessing it allows you to lord it over waiters and airline desk clerks all over the world. Hardly surprising, then, that people high in nPower are more likely to carry it.

Finally, nPower has been shown to be related to the amount of alcohol drunk by male students and businessmen, presumably because the alcohol helps them feel more powerful. Men with high needs for power also tend to be more exploitative of women, in the mini-Don Juan mould. They have more extensive sexual experience and reveal details of their sex life more readily. They prefer wives who are dependent rather than independent and their marriages are more likely to fail. To those who seek power, it seems that sex is just another conquest.

Research on nPower has followed much the same path as that on nAch, and following the earlier work outlined above has come research on nPower in women and on fear of power. Studies have also examined the relationship between the expressions of power in children's reading books and the power behaviour of countries thirty to fifty years later. The research on nPower is open to the same methodological criticisms as that on nAch, since almost all the work on individual differences and the power motive is based on the TAT, and reflects the limitations inherent in this projective technique.

And yet power has a fascination for many. Books with titles like *Power and How to Get It* regularly appear, and often become best-sellers. It is a field which psychologists are only beginning to understand, with the relatively crude instruments available, but in which important strides have already been made.

Conclusions

To some extent, this chapter on motivation has been a rag-bag of bits and pieces. We said at the beginning of the chapter that the different topics within it – interests, values, need for achievement and for power – have in common the issue of 'wants', such as what the individual wants from a job, from life and from leisure time. Yet the concept of motivation overlaps with very many areas of psychology, including memory, learning and perception, as well as individual differences. Likewise, the contents of this chapter overlap with aspects of most of the others. All the topics covered here under motivation, especially need for achievement and for power, can be seen as elements of personality, which concerned us in the previous chapter. The question of motivation also reappears in the next chapter, on assessment, since how one wants to appear or what one wants to achieve at an interview or on paper-and-pencil tests is likely to affect the result. It is as well to remind ourselves that motivation is central to many areas of individual differences and is not so tidy as to be confined to one chapter.

7 Approaches to assessment

Judging other people is a fundamental aspect of our everyday life. We continually assess how they are likely to behave, how they will react to us and how we should respond to them. And an awful lot of the time we get it wrong. There are lots of experiments showing that if you ask people to predict how other people will behave in a particular situation, they do little better than chance. Some of these experiments may be criticized on the grounds that they require subjects to make judgements about strangers – surely they would do better if they were asked about people they knew well. It seems not; Dymond (1954) asked married couples to predict their spouses' answers to a set of questions and found little difference in accuracy between happily and unhappily married couples, neither group doing much better than chance in their predictions. That we manage to live with our errors of assessment says much for our ability to rationalize after the event. We have a whole panoply of devices for deluding ourselves about the quality of our interpersonal assessments, but it is hard to disagree with Cook (1982) that much of the time people's judgements about each other are either wrong or so vague as to be unverifiable.

Some awareness of the difficulties of achieving accurate assessment inevitably does come through, and never more so than where there is a formal need to judge others and to act on those judgements. Assessing people in vocational guidance, or as part of medical or psychiatric diagnosis, selecting them for jobs or for different kinds of educational institution, all bring home to the assessor that his or her mistakes may be very costly in human terms. This sobering realization is apt to make people recognize the frailties of their own judgement and to seek some help. Enter the psychologist, doing what he is probably best known for by the general public, constructing and administering psychological tests. A large part of the population has at some time or other been confronted with a psychological test, yet paradoxically this is a topic more often subject to myths, misinformation and controversy than most others in psychology. People's beliefs about tests and their reactions to them are worth a book in themselves, and we will touch on them briefly later in this chapter. Suffice to say for the moment that they range from extreme scepticism to blind faith.

Almost from the outset, the study of individual differences has been associated with the measurement of individual differences (or psychometrics, as it is often called). So psychological tests are usually discussed in this context. However, the assessment of individuals is a wider concern than just the use of tests – it involves many other procedures, and without some appreciation of these alternatives to tests, it is impossible to evaluate the latter properly. In this chapter we will first look at psychological testing and its underlying concepts in some detail, and then move on to review the other main techniques that can be used in assessment.

Psychological tests

Basic concepts in testing

One of the fundamental qualities required of a psychological test is that it be *reliable*. Essentially, this means that the test will give the same or almost the same result when administered to an individual on two or more occasions. For example there would be little value in an intelligence test that indicated you were well above average one week, severely subnormal the next and average the third week. One should take note of two things here: we are assuming first, that the test is measuring a fairly enduring characteristic of the individual (if it were assessing moods, then marked variation in results might well be expected) and, secondly, that the scores being compared are not from testing sessions held at widely different times (over a long period even enduring characteristics of the individual will show some change).

Reliability, then, is the ability of the test to be consistent. There are a number of ways in which this degree of consistency can be assessed. The two main ones are test–retest reliability and split-half reliability. In the first of these, the test is simply given to the same group of people at two different sessions and the results are correlated. The reliability coefficient may thus be anything from −1.0 to +1.0, but for a test with good reliability one can reasonably expect something in the region of +0.8 to 0.9. Just how much time should be left between one testing session and another is a matter of judgement. Clearly, it cannot be too long, for the reason indicated above. Although there are no rules as such, it is often suggested that a period of 2–4 weeks is about right. This is long enough for people to have forgotten the test items (though there may be some practice effect) but too short a time for any major change in their personalities or abilities to have taken place. The other approach, split-half reliability, involves dividing the test into two equal halves and comparing the scores for the two halves. The division will often be on the basis of odd and even numbered items. Since all are supposed to be measuring the same thing, you should find a high correlation between the two scores. Usually, the two parts of the test have been taken together and as far as the subject is concerned, it is just one testing session. Split-half reliability is a measure of the internal consistency of the test and one would normally want to establish both kinds of reliability in evaluating a test.

Reliability in a test is necessary, but not of itself enough. There is nothing to say that a test may not be consistent in being wrong. After all, at one point in history there was a very high reliability within and between individuals in the judgement that the earth was flat. Apart from being reliable, an assessment procedure has to have *validity*. The validity of a test can refer to various aspects of its use and definition, but basically boils down to whether the test actually does measure what it purports to measure. The reader may like to pause here for a moment and think about how he or she would establish a test's validity.

The chief types of validity are:

1 *Face validity*: the personality quizzes that most people have come across in magazines ('How considerate a partner are

you?', 'Are you a good neighbour?', etc.) have high face validity – that is they look as if they are measuring what they say they are. However, it is no wiser to judge a test by its appearance than it is to judge a book by its cover – face validity guarantees nothing. It is worth having, then? To answer that question, imagine how you would feel if you went for a job as a teacher and were required to take a test that involved making a series of preference choices between colours presented to you. You might well think that this was irrelevant to the job, a meaningless task, and you might feel rather alienated. Had you been given a straightforward personality questionnaire instead, you may well have seen this as a reasonable device for trying to screen out neurotic or unstable individuals from the job. So a test with face validity is often more acceptable to those being tested – but the other side of the coin is that as its function is more obvious it is also easier to manipulate to deliberately give the impression you think is wanted. We will return to this problem later.

2 *Content validity*: this requires a detailed analysis of the skills measured by the test and the skills involved in the performance of the job or task. At its most simple, a spelling test samples a child's spelling, or a reaction-time test measures reaction time. In a more realistic context, an analysis of the job of police officer might reveal that powers of observation and of memory were highly important to effectiveness in that job; thus a test of such powers would have content validity for the job.

3 *External validation*: sometimes known as correlational validity because it refers to the practice of correlating test results with some external measure of the attribute being assessed. For example, a test of mechanical aptitude might be given to a group of engineering apprentices and their scores correlated with their supervisors' ratings of how well they were doing in their training; the high-test-scorers would be expected to be the ones doing best in the view of the supervisors. This is an example of *concurrent* external validation, the test results being correlated with some present measure of behaviour. With *predictive* external validation, using the same example, the apprentices' test scores might be matched up subsequently with the final assessment given to them at the end of their apprenticeship. In this case, the test results are validated against a performance measure taken some time later.

External validation is considered very important indeed for psychological tests, but inherent in it is a major problem. The performance measure that the tests are validated against, called the 'criterion', may or may not be a good measure of the quality you are assessing. If you are validating an intelligence test against examination results, how good a measure of intelligence are examination results? Or if you try to validate the tests used in selecting people for management posts by using criteria such as their annual performance ratings and their subsequent promotions, can you be sure that these in their turn are an accurate reflection of merit? Most of the criteria used in validating tests have their imperfections, and it is important to remember this; the validity of the test can only be as high as the validity of the criterion!

4 *Construct validation*: psychologists are often trying to measure constructs such as anxiety or self-esteem which are theoretical abstractions. Such qualities are inferred from behaviour, and have no 'real' existence in the sense that, say, the weight and height of an individual have. One way of validating measures of such constructs is to see if they make scientific and conceptual sense. To put it another way, construct validation means testing the theory that lies behind the test. A good example would be Eysenck's concept of extraversion. In this theory, Eysenck suggests that extraverts differ from introverts in the excitation–inhibition balance of the reticular system, leading to differences in conditionability, which in turn leads to the differences in behaviour we typically associate with introverts and extraverts. Thus, if we find that people who score high or low on Eysenck's questionnaire measure of extraversion do indeed show conditionability differences in the direction predicted, this establishes construct validity for the test. In this way, the test and the theory derive mutual support. Relatively few psychological tests can claim to have this kind of validity.

Any worthwhile psychological test has to have both reliability and validity (preferably external or construct validity). Note that while an unreliable test cannot be valid, reliability does not ensure validity, as we pointed out earlier. Having outlined these basic concepts in testing, we will now look briefly at how psychological tests are constructed.

Test construction

Let us take a questionnaire measure of neuroticism as an example. The first thing to do is to gather a series of items (i.e. questions) that seem appropriate. There are two major ways of doing this. The first, which can be called theoretical keying, involves the test constructor in writing a large number of items that seem likely to tap neuroticism; they may be chosen on the basis of a theory or on intuition. The items would be given to a group of neurotic subjects and the relationship between the items would be examined. Those items that do not seem to be grouped with the others would be deleted, on the ground that if items are measuring the same thing they should be associated (correlated) with one another. Factor-analytic techniques are now often used to establish the homogeneity of the test items. The whole procedure should be repeated and the pool of test items further refined. The Kuder Preference Record is an example of a test constructed with this approach.

The other way of choosing test items is called empirical keying (or criterion-keying). Here the items do not have to be seen to relate to the quality being measured. You might collect a large number of items and then give them to a group of neurotics and a group of emotionally stable individuals. Any item that the groups tend to respond to differently is retained, while any item that does not discriminate between the two groups is rejected. This is a severely pragmatic technique. Any consideration as to *why* items do or do not discriminate is superfluous, the main thing being that they do. The Strong Vocational Interest Blank is an example of empirical keying.

Quite apart from these general strategies for selection of items, any item has to be edited for clarity, length, style, bias and other things, none of which we have space to go into here. The reader is referred to Anastasi (1982) for a full treatment of the subject. Assuming, however, that our items for the neuroticism question-naire have been through all the preliminary stages, the next step will be to look at the reliability and validity of the questionnaire. The way of assessing the first of these is evident from the previous section. As far as validity is concerned, any test based on empirical-keying will tend to have less face validity than one based on theoretical keying. But elements of the empirical-keying tech-nique are often present in the external validation of tests derived by other means. For example, a questionnaire measure of neuro-ticism based on theoretically keyed items may well be given to groups of hospitalized neurotics and emotionally stable indi-viduals as part of the validation process – discriminating between them would provide concurrent validity. The differentiation of neurotics and non-neurotics is a rather crude one, and so the test constructor might seek further concurrent validation by correlating the scores on the neuroticism questionnaire with clinicians' ratings of the degree of neuroticism shown by each individual in a group of psychiatric out-patients. Readers might like to think for themselves how to go about establishing the *predictive* validity of the questionnaire – though it has to be said that this time-consuming step is unfortunately not always taken in constructing tests.

When a test has been through all these stages satisfactorily, there is a need to develop norms for it. If a person gets a score of 52 on a test whose scores can range from 0 to 80, it does not tell you very much. What you need to know is how other people tend to score on the test. If you find that the average score for neurotics is 50, while for non-neurotic individuals the average score is 20, you are in a better position to interpret the individual's score. This is what test norms provide – information about the scoring pattern of relevant groups (relevant, that is, to the purpose of the test). To be of any real value the norms have to be based on quite large samples. Another procedure often followed to facilitate interpretation of test results is to standardize the raw scores, i.e. fit them to a normal distribution. Many intelligence tests, for example, have a mean of 100 and a standard deviation of 15. Thus, a person with a score of 122 is between one and two standard units above the mean, and is, therefore, in the top 16 per cent of the population.

In this short description of the major steps in test construction much has been omitted. There has been no discussion of item difficulty, base rates, selection ratios and numerous other topics. Some further aspects of test development will surface in the following pages, but it is hoped that enough has been said to illustrate the thought and care that goes into devising a psychological test. Readers will judge for themselves whether an equivalent amount of effort and sophistication is to be found in other, alternative selection devices. One final point needs to be made here. Implicit in the above discussion is an essential characteristic of tests – they are *objectively scored*. The feelings or views of the person scoring the testing cannot affect the score obtained by the subject in the way that, for example, the different predilections of two judges in a beauty contest might influence their assessments of the contestants. This does not, of course, mean that there can be no variation in the interpretation of what the scores imply.

There are more than 2000 psychological tests published in the USA and Britain; this particular 'industry' seems to be growing. It is not the intention here to go through them – that would take this book and more. We will just briefly describe two of the main categories and quote one or two examples of the best-known tests of each type (for a comprehensive listing, see Buros 1974).

Individual and group tests of mental ability   On page 11, the original concept of IQ was described. The formula

$$IQ = \frac{MA}{CA} \times 100$$

is not one that finds favour in modern tests of intelligence, not least because when mental age reaches a maximum for an individual, his or her chronological age is likely to go on increasing for many years. The effect is to produce an ever increasing figure for the bottom part of the IQ equation while the top part stays static, with the result that the IQ will steadily deteriorate, irrespective of whether the individual's actual performance on the test remains the same. This does not seem either sensible or helpful, and so most intelligence tests now rest on the concept of deviation IQ. This is the practice described in the preceding section of standardizing scores. The average IQ score for a particular age group is set at 100 and the individual's score just expresses the extent to which his or her performance on the test deviates from this. Thus, a person is compared to other people in the same age group, and over time, whilst some aspects of his or her intellectual functioning will deteriorate and others improve, the person will remain in much the same position relative to his or her peers.

Deviation IQ is used in the widely employed Wechsler Adult Intelligence Scale (WAIS). This presents the same items to all age groups, the standards of performance varying with each age level. Maintaining a consistency of item type is important as it ensures that you are measuring comparable abilities at each age (the original Binet test failed to do this). The WAIS contains both verbal and non-verbal, or 'performance', items. Wechsler felt, correctly, that intelligence is not just a verbal phenomenon and this had to be reflected in his test. Non-verbal test items are generally found to be less affected by the educational level or social class of those tested. Examples of the kinds of performance test items used in the WAIS and other tests are given in figure 5.

Block design
Put the blocks together to make the picture

Object assembly
Put the pieces together as quickly as you can to make the picture

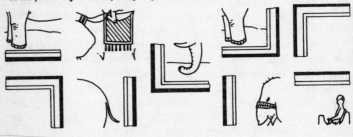

Figure 5 Performance test items like those used in the Wechsler Adult Intelligence Scale. (After Baron, Byrne and Kantowitz, 1980, p. 435)

The WAIS is an individual test of ability developed in the USA, and there are tests specifically for younger age groups which Wechsler devised on the same broad lines (the Wechsler Intelligence Scale for Children, WISC, and the Wechsler Pre-School and Primary Scale of Intelligence, WPPSI). The more recently produced British Ability Scales are very much more complex. Designed to cover the age range 2½ to 17, they consist of 23 scales divided into 6 major areas: speed of information processing, reasoning, spatial imagery, perceptual matching, short-term memory, and retrieval and application of knowledge. These include verbal and non-verbal items, and the intention is that all the scales can be used or specific ones can be selected for specialized assessments. The British Ability Scales are very comprehensive, and flexible in use (Elliott *et al.* 1983).

Individual tests tend to be fairly time-consuming affairs. The advent of the First World War led the Americans to develop group tests of intelligence that could be administered quickly and to large numbers of army recruits. These were a great success and since then group tests of intelligence have burgeoned. They may consist of verbal, numerical or non-verbal (diagrammatic) items, or of all these. Some of the most widely used in Britain are the AH series, devised by Alice Heim. The AH6, for example, is a high-level test of general ability used in selecting amongst groups for managerial posts. The total administration time may be up to sixty-five minutes, and the test comes in two forms, one more suitable for those with a predominantly arts education and one for people with a scientific background (Heim, 1970).

The tests mentioned so far are of general ability, though they can in varying degrees be broken down to give scores of more specific abilities. Other tests set out from the start to measure individual types of ability, particularly as they relate to the individual's capacity to acquire skills and knowledge for certain jobs or classes of jobs. Such tests are called aptitude tests. They may be designed for a particular purpose, such as the Modern Language Aptitude Test (which seeks to predict success in learning a foreign language) and the Computer Programming Aptitude Battery. Others, like the Multiple Aptitude Test, try to assess a range of aptitudes, such as clerical speed and accuracy, mechanical reasoning and numerical ability.

Personality and interest inventories   The measures described here involve questionnaires and check lists of one kind or another.

Some psychologists would prefer not to talk of them as 'tests' because there are no right or wrong answers as such, and so they are not tests in the sense that intelligence tests are. However, in the normal run of things they are grouped together – at least in the public's mind – and are constructed on the same general principles. Personality inventories consist of series of questions like 'Do you feel confident of yourself in social situations?', 'Do you like to have the last word?', 'Do you sometimes feel down for no reason at all?' and so on. The subject is given a limited choice of response to each item, often just Yes/No or True/False. The questions normally centre on behaviour, preferences, feelings and moods. Some of the best-known examples have already been mentioned in connection with the work of Cattell and Eysenck. Perhaps the most famous of them is the Minnesota Multiphasic Personality Inventory (MMPI), a blockbuster of 558 items measuring 9 clinically oriented scales such as paranoia and hysteria. This criterion-keyed test has served as an item pool for the construction of many other shorter tests (e.g. the Taylor Manifest Anxiety Scale).

Interest inventories are, as their name implies, aimed at discovering what an individual's interests are – social, artistic or creative, mechanical, etc. The ulterior purpose, however, is to assess motivation. The notion behind interest inventories is that there is a strong relationship between what people are interested in and what they like doing, what they are motivated towards. Examples of well-established interest measures are the Kuder Vocational Preference Record, Holland's Vocational Preference Inventory and the Rothwell–Miller Interest Bank. As you might gather from these names, interest inventories are frequently used in the occupational counselling field to assist people in making career choices.

Attitudes and reactions to taking psychological tests

A very important practical requirement in the use of psychological tests is that they should be administered under standardized conditions. All extraneous factors that might affect the individual's performance on a test should be controlled for, much as if the test were an experiment (which in some cases it is). This generally means making sure that the lighting, temperature and noise levels are all within an acceptable range. These cannot be arranged in advance by the test constructor – it is up to whoever is using the test to ensure that the right conditions pertain. What the test constructor *can* do is to provide a standard set of instructions to be read to those taking the test, so that everyone is presented with exactly the same clear directions as to what they are to do. The test administrator has to read these instructions in a neutral voice – though there is obviously some room for variation here unless one uses a standard, typed set of instructions.

While you can control for the testing conditions up to a point, you cannot control for the reactions of those taking the tests. Anyone who has done a psychological test can probably remember how they felt. One of the major problems is that of Test Anxiety. This is a fairly common phenomenon where the individual, instead of just getting on with the test, makes non-task-relevant responses, for example sits there thinking about how much better everybody else is doing, and contemplating the disastrous consequences of failing the test. Such people, if given the test under conditions where there is no valued outcome depending on their performance, characteristically perform far more effectively than they do if something does depend on their results. Test Anxiety is a well-documented and much studied psychological reaction, and it can be treated effectively with behaviour therapy or cognitive therapy (or a mixture of both). However, much of the time all that can be done about it is for test administrators to be on the look-out for individuals who are exhibiting signs of distress when taking tests and to investigate the reasons for this either then or later. The results of these investigations can be taken account of in evaluating test results.

A quite different problem in the use of tests arises from deliberate distortion or faking on the part of those tested. The most obvious example of circumstances where this is likely to happen is when personality inventories are used in job selection. Poppleton (1975) found that applicants for the job of salesman scored higher on extraversion and lower on anxiety – as measured by Cattell's 16PF – than did salesmen already employed. The latter were already more extraverted and less anxious than the general population, and it seems likely that the applicants presented themselves on the questionnaire in such a way as to give the impression of being the sort of people the selectors were looking for. There is plenty of other evidence of this kind. Perhaps less obviously, there are also quite a few studies showing that psychiatric patients have a variety of motives in assessment situations and that they can and do deliberately manipulate the image they present of themselves on tests (Shackleton and Fletcher, 1973). To combat the possibility of faking, the test constructor has two main weapons. One is to employ criterion-keying, which sometimes makes it much less clear to the candidate what the aim of the test is and thus more difficult to dissimulate. The other is to incorporate a lie-scale. These, which are often used, consist of items like 'I never lose my temper': True/False. Most people will honestly reply 'False', and anyone who does not is probably either lying or totally lacking in insight. It *could* just be the case that you have a very over-controlled person who genuinely never does lose his or her temper. But after responding similarly to a string of such items, you would conclude either that this person was lying or that you had a *bona fide* saint on your hands. Given the renowned supply shortage of the latter, you would probably settle for the former conclusion. Lie-scale items, unfortunately, tend to be rather transparent and anyone with a reasonable degree of intelligence might be expected to spot most of them.

A close relative of deliberate faking is social desirability. This is the tendency of a subject to endorse an item according to how socially desirable he or she perceives it to be. Although this means that the person is conveying a 'good' picture of him- or herself, it is not quite the same as faking. First, it may occur without any overtly motivating aspects in the testing situation – the individual is not seeking to achieve some specific goal through creating a false impression. Secondly, it may not be altogether conscious on the subject's part. Most of the original work on this concept was done by A.C. Edwards, and in his own test (the Edwards Personal Preference Schedule) the problem is dealt with by having subjects choose between items that have been carefully balanced in terms of social desirability. For those constructing and using tests, social desirability is one of a group of hazards known as response sets. These are stylistic consistencies generated by the form of the response, and as such are mostly unconscious distortions. One of the main ones is acquiescence, a tendency to accept any personality statement as applying to oneself (or the opposite, rejecting all of them); the subject tends to say 'Yes' to everything regardless of content. This can have serious consequences for the validity of tests, unless controlled. For example, a high acquiescence set on the MMPI will tend to make the individual appear highly abnormal or psychotic (though there may well be some genuine connection between acquiescence and deviant personality characteristics as well). There are various ways of dealing with the acquiescence set, such as balancing the number of 'Yes' and 'No' items in a test, but none seems entirely satisfactory. Response sets in general remain a problem in test construction.

Issues in psychological testing

Some of the difficulties and controversies concerning both the construction and the use of tests have been mentioned already in this chapter, and appear elsewhere in the book. Perhaps the most notable of these is the question of whether psychological tests discriminate unfairly against minority groups, an issue touched on both directly and indirectly in chapter 3. There are several possible sources of such discrimination. First, there may be bias in the content of a test. For example, some test items require the individual to identify correctly the meaning of proverbs. This may be all well and good for those raised in white, middle-class families, where they will probably have come across similar sayings. For people of a different cultural background, though, the chances of success can be much reduced by their unfamiliarity with Western proverbs. In fact any test of a verbal nature is likely to disadvantage individuals from less educated or culturally different backgrounds. Unfortunately, constructing non-verbal tests does not seem to be a solution for all of these problems either, perhaps because members of some minority groups are less sophisticated in their test-taking strategies and differ in their attitude towards and motivation in testing.

Another criticism often levelled against intelligence tests specifically is that they only test convergent thinking, and that some people can get the 'wrong' answer on a test because they have construed the question in a different light from the one intended; the answer given is correct if viewed in the context of their unorthodox, perhaps more creative, interpretation. There is some justification in this charge, but this kind of thing does not seem to occur very often – or at least, it does not often come to light. It seems unlikely, too, that anyone would go through a whole test giving this kind of answer; it is more likely that it would occur on one or two items only, which would have little consequence since any reliable test is likely to have a large number of items. Another, wider question is whether ability tests show practice effects. Anastasi (1982) reports a number of studies showing that significant gains are made by individuals on their test scores when given equivalent forms of tests either in immediate succession or with intervening periods of up to three years. In fact, extensive test-taking experience gives an individual an advantage over test-inexperienced people generally, not just on the same test. The reader may like to keep this in mind and see what experience of test-taking can be obtained as a useful investment for future job-hunting. The important thing is to become familiar with ability-test items and to increase one's confidence in handling them. Some tests try as far as possible to negate this effect by providing quite lengthy sets of examples that have to be done by all subjects first. Short orientation and practice sessions can be quite effective in 'levelling' the test sophistication of the subjects.

Much of what has been said so far relates to the fairness and adequacy of tests. Other concerns centre on the people using tests and what they do with the findings from them. In both Britain and the USA attempts are made to stop psychological tests falling into the hands of people not qualified to use them. Unfortunately, these efforts do not always succeed. It is mainly when tests are used by non-psychologists that their results tend to be given far too much weight, and in many cases to be misinterpreted as well. Lay people also have an unfortunate habit of not bothering to look too closely into the test's background. A senior executive in a consultancy firm once proclaimed about a new test that he was not interested in 'boring validity studies', and that he had a 'gut feeling' that this test worked. With such variation in the quality of the users, it is no surprise to find that there is some anxiety about the confidentiality of test results. Who should be allowed to see them, or keep a record of them? Should the individual be asked for permission to give the results to a third party? Should the person taking the test be told the results? You might like to stop a moment and think about your position on such questions – what are the pros and cons? In the USA particularly, there is a growing feeling that individuals should be informed about the purpose of tests, how their results will be used and their availability to others when the tests are given in an institutional context (courts, colleges, industry, etc.). There is also an increasing willingness in some settings to give people access to their own results and to share the interpretation process with them; this is common practice in vocational counselling and may spread to some selection situations too. However, it does require a high level of skill not only to communicate a correct and non-technical account of the test findings but also to help the individual confront the strengths and weaknesses of his or her performance. It would definitely not be a good idea just to give individuals their test scores without guidance on interpretation.

There are many other aspects of the debate on test scores. For example: have the parents and the teachers the right to see the scores when a child is tested? How long should the test scores be kept on record? Policies are only gradually evolving. Two things are certain, however: psychometric tests are here to stay, and the controversies about them will continue.

Other approaches to assessment

The variety of methods that have been used in attempting to assess people testifies to the complexity and difficulty of the task. In briefly reviewing them here, the same broad concepts of reliability and validity that were discussed in relation to tests will be applied to these other techniques; in other words, do they produce consistent assessments and do they actually measure what they purport to measure?

The interview

This is without doubt the best-known and most widely used method of assessment despite the fact that since the 1920s there has been a string of research findings indicating that (as normally practised) it is a method of doubtful quality. All too frequently interviewers disagree among themselves on the assessments given – the reliability of the interview is low, then, as different applications of it to the same person produce varying assessments. This means that its validity must also be poor, and research has indeed shown this to be the case; for example, one study demonstrated that you could have predicted students' degree results some years hence just as well by picking them out of a hat as by the interviewers' assessments!

Much research has gone into trying to discover the reasons for this low effectiveness. One of the main sources of unreliability is that untrained interviewers approach the interview in an unsystematic way, so that they often collect different kinds of information and not surprisingly come to different judgements based on it. Training interviewers and providing them with a planned approach to the task improves the quality of the assessment considerably (see Bayne, 1982, for an interesting account of some

99

of the evidence on this). However, even ensuring that interviewers get the same information does not guarantee that they will all interpret it in the same way. One of the many distorting factors in interview judgements is that they are often probably based as much on *how* the interviewee says things as on *what* is said. Dipboye and Wiley showed in a series of studies (1977, 1978) that not only did interviewers of candidates for a managerial position rate those with a moderately aggressive self-presentation style more favourably than those with a more passive style, but they also rated the latter as significantly more emotionally unstable and illogical despite the fact that the *content* of the interviewees' responses had been controlled for and was the same in both cases! So judgements were influenced by the way the candidate presented himself. Since candidates have widely varying ideas on how to tackle interviews (Fletcher, 1981a), this is going to be an important source of error in interviewers' judgements. Candidates can presumably help themselves a lot in avoiding these kinds of errors on the interviewers' part by preparing themselves properly beforehand and knowing what *not* to do in interviews (Fletcher, 1981b).

There is a very considerable volume of research on the interview process (see Arvey and Campion, 1982, for a review). Later studies in this field suggest that under certain conditions the interview does have something to offer. However, as it is normally carried out it remains a selection device of low reliability and validity.

Self-assessment

Both interviews and personality questionnaires rest on the individual's self-report, and so why can we not go the whole hog and just ask people directly to assess themselves? The two main objections to this have been that they are not able to assess themselves (either through simple lack of insight or, in Freudian theory, because of the inaccessibility of the unconscious) and that in many situations they would be motivated to enhance their self-assessment. However, the evidence is that accuracy of both the individual's own assessment of present performance and predictions of future performance compare very favourably with other approaches in many circumstances (Shrauger and Osberg, 1981; Mabe and West, 1982). Since people can self-assess, the question is whether they are willing to do so honestly in situations where there may be something to be gained by presenting a good image.

It is probably safer to assume they are not; most of the evidence points this way. But the potential value of self-assessment has almost certainly been understated, and more knowledge is needed of differences in individual capacities for it and of the conditions that promote it. In some settings, for instance vocational counselling, the motivation of the individual is not a problem, and elements of self-assessment have been good practice for some time now. It is possible that the technique could be extended into job-selection procedures if used carefully and alongside other assessment devices.

Neophenomenological techniques

These are approaches to assessment that concentrate on deriving a picture of how individuals view themselves and their world. They are essentially idiographic in nature, with some modification, though they can be used to compare people. The best known and most widely used of them is the repertory grid (described on pp. 60–2). Just one other technique will be mentioned here. This is the Q-sort. There are variations in how it is used, but typically the individual would be presented with a series of up to a hundred cards on each of which is printed a statement, for example 'I am quite an anxious person', 'I get on with people very easily'. After reading through all the cards, the person is asked to place the card with the statement most like him or her at one end of a table and the card with the statement least like them at the other end. Then they are asked to select the three cards with the statements next most like and next least like them, and to place these alongside the cards they have already put on the table. Gradually, all the cards and statements are sorted in this way into nine piles approximating to a normal distribution, with fewest cards at the extremes and most cards in the middle (being midway between 'mostlike' and 'leastlike' the person). This would be called a 'self-sort'. Doing the same thing but asking the individual to sort the cards in terms of 'most like I would like to be' and 'least like I would like to be' would give an 'ideal self-sort'. By numbering the cards it is possible to correlate the two sorts done by an individual, thus giving a measure of the congruence between perceived self and ideal self. Rogers and Dymond (1954) did this and found that in client-centred therapy, patients' increasing self-acceptance was reflected in a higher correlation of self- and ideal self-sorts at the end of the treatment than existed at the beginning. The Q-sort, like the repertory grid, is quite a time-consuming procedure, but can be valuable, albeit for a limited range of purposes.

Work-sample tests

These involve individuals in performing a task or series of tasks that are thought to have direct, central relevance to the job they are being selected for. In some cases, the tasks may be actual samples of the work to be performed by the job-holder. They may involve psychomotor tasks, like using a sewing machine or exercising some keyboard skills. Or they may focus on how the individual copes with complex decision-making under time pressure, as in the in-tray exercise. Here, the candidate has to work through a set of problems of the kind that any manager might find in his in-tray (on a rather bad day!). How this is coped with in the time allowed throws light on the person's judgement, analytical ability, written expression, and so on.

Work-sample tests can be devised to assess aspects of group functioning too. A common variant is the committee exercise, in which a group of candidates is given a problem or series of problems which they have to solve as a committee. Each candidate may take it in turn to 'chair' the committee as it deals with problem.

Work-sample tests are in many cases quite costly in time and effort, and tend to be specific to assessments done for a particular purpose. Within those limitations, though, they look very promising and their validity compares favourably with alternative approaches, including psychological tests (Robertson and Kandola, 1982).

Physiological measures

Although there may be some relationships between such physiological measures as electroencephalogram readings, or indicators of autonomic nervous system reactivity, and personality, they are not well understood and this is not an approach used outside the research setting. There is one important exception to this – the polygraph, or lie-detector. Amongst other things this measures galvanic skin response (GSR). When the individual experiences an emotional response to some stimulus, part of that response is a set of physiological changes orchestrated by the autonomic nervous system. One of these is an increase in the electrical conductivity of the skin (or, in other words, sweating). Very small increases in GSR can be measured by applying electrodes to the skin, and the notion is that when an individual tells lies under interrogation this will involve some slight emotional reaction and hence a change in GSR. This technique is widely used in the USA, not least by the CIA, though psychologists seldom seem to be responsible for it. Under certain conditions and in connection with particular methods, the lie-detector can be useful. But more generally it should be regarded with great caution and even scepticism; the rate at which it identifies truthful people incorrectly as liars is too high for comfort (Lykken, 1981).

Projective techniques

Often classified as psychological tests, projective techniques are not usually developed in the same systematic and careful way as tests, nor in most cases are they objectively scored. They are thus perhaps better called 'techniques' than tests. The rationale for them is that if you present individuals with a vague stimulus and ask them to interpret it, to make sense of it in some way, they will 'project' important aspects of their personality into the interpretation. The most famous examples of projective techniques are the Rorschach, in which the subject has to make interpretative responses to ink blots, and the Thematic Apperception Test (TAT, see chapter 6), where a series of pictures of scenes is presented and the subject is requested to make up a story as to what is happening in them. Most of these techniques are subjectively scored and lack any clear guidance on their interpretation. Their reliability and validity is extremely variable and they seem very susceptible to extraneous influences, such as the warmth of the personality of the person giving them. (For a full consideration of their drawbacks, see Vernon, 1964.) Although almost synonymous with the public image of psychology, they are relatively little used now; like the 'depth' theories of personality with which they were associated, they have had their day.

Conclusions

In this second section, some of the alternative assessment approaches to psychometric tests have been briefly described.

There are many others – non-verbal behaviour and expressive movement, biographical data, peer ratings, graphology (handwriting analysis), etc. For some of the less conventional approaches, such as astrology, the reader is referred to Mackenzie Davey and Harris (1982) for a proper evaluation. Of the ones looked at here, few if any are developed as systematically as are psychological tests. As far as achieving satisfactory levels of reliability and validity is concerned, projective techniques, physiological measures and interviews (as they are normally carried out) are not in the same league as tests. Under some conditions, self-assessment may be an effective alternative to psychological tests, and, in their limited range of application, work-sample tests may be even better. The neophenomenological techniques, being orientated more towards idiographic use, are less appropriate for comparison.

Looking at the relative merits of the different techniques from the viewpoint of reliability and validity does, of course, oversimplify the issue. As we will see in chapter 9, often the best results are achieved by combining the various approaches. They do not all yield the same kind of information, and to get a broad picture of the individual more than one technique is required. There are also the questions of their advantages and disadvantages in terms of cost and of the reactions of those being assessed, neither of which can be overlooked. Just as there are those who complain – often rightly – of the bias and subjectivity of interviews, there are others who resent taking tests 'because they reduce me to a number'. Whatever the approach to assessment used, it is desirable that the people assessed feel they have been treated fairly and given a chance to do justice to themselves.

$\mathcal{8}$ Group differences

The very process of examining differences between individuals means that we can group similar individuals together and examine differences between those groups. The most obvious difference is between men and women, but some of the other group differences that have interested psychologists have been race and age. This chapter looks at each of these three groups in turn to ask the questions: What differences, if any, exist between one group and another? What are the causes of these differences?

Sex differences

The psychological differences between men and women are fascinating to lay people. It is probably because we are all one or the other – men or women – and so can readily identify with the topic. It also has a considerable fascination and importance for psychologists. 'No topic in psychology is of more perennial interest,' remarks Tyler in her book *The Psychology of Human Differences* (1965); and Maccoby and Jacklin (1975) reviewed over 2000 articles and books on the subject. We can only provide a short summary of all this work, and readers who agree about its fascination and importance are referred to Maccoby and Jacklin's classic work for more detail. We will cover three areas of research work on sex differences: cognitive abilities, aggression and dependency. Then we will look at some of the explanations for these differences.

Cognitive abilities

The general intelligence, or IQ score, of males and females is very much the same. The Scottish Council for Research in Education in 1939 collected one of the best samples of intelligence-test scores in this sort of research. They found no evidence that one sex was superior to the other in overall intelligence. This is hardly surprising. Even if differences existed we would be unlikely to know, since tests of intelligence have been standardized to minimize or eliminate sex differences.

Differences on more specific abilities are another story. Research has shown that from an early age girls are better than boys in most aspects of verbal performance. Before they can speak, girl babies are more responsive to the speech of adults. Girls start to speak, on average, earlier than boys and have fewer speech defects. Girls learn to read sooner than boys and twice as many boys are retarded readers. Throughout the secondary-school years, girls do better on tests of grammar, spelling and word fluency. It is verbal fluency in which they excel; they are no better than boys at verbal comprehension and verbal reasoning, such as analogies. Girls also tend to do better in tests of creativity, which of course involve the use of language. But a recent, intriguing finding is that the gap between the sexes in verbal ability seems to be narrowing. Research reports in both Britain and the USA indicate that the verbal ability gap is smaller than it was twenty-five years ago (Wittig and Petersen, 1978). Why this should be is a mystery. It could be due to new more intrinsically interesting reading books for young children. This might be encouraging boys to take more time and effort over learning to read. It might also be due to the slow but continuing breakdown in sex-role stereotyping. One explanation for boys' lack of verbal ability used to be that boys saw reading as a girlish activity, as sissyish. Perhaps teachers and parents are slowly (and unconsciously?) breaking down this image.

With mathematical ability, male superiority is the rule. It shows up around the age of 11 on tests that require mathematical reasoning rather than on those that require simple computations. It may be, again, that maths is seen as a 'masculine' subject and so girls are not attracted to it. Instead, they go for the verbal subjects such as languages and literature.

The fact that maths, especially geometry, has a high spatial component, must also be a reason why men do better than women, since boys also do better on visual-spatial tasks. These test the ability to visualize and manipulate objects in space. Figure 6 shows an example. This is often given as part of the reason why boys do better at school at physics, science and mechanical subjects, and why men dominate in engineering, architecture, mechanical design, painting, and so on.

Sex differences have also been found in a cognitive style called 'field independence'. A cognitive style is an individual's consistent way of approaching or dealing with information, that is the strategies people employ in dealing with information around them. A field-independent person keeps the different parts of a

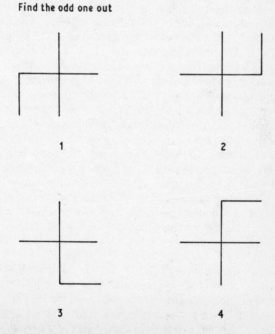

Find the odd one out

1   2

3   4

Figure 6   A visual-spatial test item. (After Eysenck, 1966)

situation separate from one another and ignores aspects of a situation that are irrelevant at that moment. Such people are active in dealing with their environment and in controlling their impulses. The field-dependent person, on the other hand, reacts to a situation as a whole rather than analysing it into its components. Such a person tends to accept the environment and reacts to it in a global, intuitive, passive way.

One method used in research on these styles is the Embedded Figures Test, where a subject has to find a simple shape embedded in a more complex one. Figure 7 provides an example. You must try to suppress your response to the figure on the right as a whole, and find that part of it which corresponds to the more simple figure on the left. From the age of about 17, males do consistently better than females. They also do better on a similar measure, the Rod and Frame Test. Here, a rod within a frame is projected on to a wall of a darkened room. The subject is asked to use a lever to move the rod into a vertical position as the frame is tilted. Again, a subject must try to ignore the tilted frame and concentrate on the rod. What these and other similar techniques get at is an individual's way of dealing with confusing information, of being able to differentiate parts of the situation and keep them separately in mind. Simply put, they look at how analytical someone is. It has been suggested as a result of these experiments that men are more field-independent, better able to think analytically. Further research shows that this may be a wrong conclusion. When a task involves touch to make or reconstruct figures, such as when a subject is shown a matchstick figure and asked to make a different figure by removing or changing the matches, men are no better than women. Similarly, women are just as good as men when asked to listen to one voice and ignore a second voice. This, like the Embedded Figures and the Rod and Frame Tests, involves separating a stimulus from its background. Only the mode of presentation of the stimulus has been changed, from seeing to hearing. So we can conclude that it is the visual-spatial component that distinguishes men from women, not their general analytical ability.

Women do well in other cognitive abilities. Most studies agree that females excel in rote memory, that is in tasks which require the exact repetition of digits, words and geometric figures. They also shine at the quick perception of details. And in tasks involving manual dexterity – light, deft, swift movements of the hands – the advantage is again with girls and women. There are difficulties in

Figure 7   An item in the Embedded Figures Test.

making absolute generalizations about this sort of ability, however, since the dexterities have been found to be highly specific. A person who is skilful at one type of movement may be below average on another. Tests commonly used to predict success in various occupations requiring dexterity highlight women *averaging* consistently higher scores than men.

To summarize, males on average are superior in mathematical reasoning and spatial relationships. Females are generally superior in verbal fluency, rote memory, perceptual speed and dexterity. These differences are apparent from the age of 11 and have practical consequences. For example, Sauls and Larson (1975), in a study which involved almost a million students throughout the USA, showed that not only do psychological tests indicate male–female differences in intellectual function, but these are also apparent when their actual school performance is compared. Boys do better at maths, the sciences and technical subjects. Girls do better at verbal subjects such as languages, literature and history.

It is important to emphasize that these are group differences, based on averages. The variability around the average is so large and the differences between the sexes so small that it is quite possible for individuals of either sex to contradict the general tendency. In a classroom it is likely that some boys will be better than the majority of girls at vocabulary, just as some girls will excel in mathematics or spatial abilities. Just because the average man has better visual-spatial ability than the average woman, it does not follow that *this* man is better than *that* woman. It is irrelevant when making decisions about *individual* men and women, such as who should be offered a place as a student architect. Something like 25 per cent of women do better than the average man on the visual-spatial questions of IQ tests. A major review of sex differences in motor, spatial and linguistic abilities (Fairweather, 1976) concluded that sex differences were outweighed by other factors such as the sex of the experimenter, and the age and culture of the subject.

Aggression

We now turn from cognitive behaviour to personality and social behaviour. Aggression is the most marked difference between the sexes in this area. The overall finding is that boys and men are more aggressive than girls and women, very much in accordance with the prevailing stereotype. These differences can be seen as early as the age of 3, with boys showing a greater tendency towards rough-and-tumble play than girls. Physical and antisocial aggression such as physical quarrels, fights, and 'negativistic' behaviour (e.g. negative attention-seeking) are more prevalent among boys than girls. These findings seem to be common in many cultures, not just our own.

In adulthood, men commit considerably more aggressive crimes than women. However, much depends upon the situation. In crimes of violence against children within the family, like child-battering, wives and husbands have fairly similar crime statistics. And girls seem to be catching up with boys. In crimes of violence committed by people under 17 years of age, the proportion committed by girls rose from 1.3 per cent in 1950 to 16 per cent in 1977 (Nicholson, 1979). However, crime statistics as a source of evidence of aggressive behaviour are highly suspect because they represent *detected* antisocial behaviour. Proportional changes in female crime may reflect changes in policemen's, magistrates' and judges' willingness to apprehend and convict females as much as changes in females' behaviour. Whatever the trends, though, males undoubtedly still commit far more crimes of violence than women.

Self-concepts concerning aggression also differentiate the sexes. When asked to rate themselves, males from the age of 15 saw themselves as more directly and overtly aggressive (Nicholson, 1979).

Just as in humans, so in non-human primates, like the chimpanzee and rhesus monkey, males show more rough-and-tumble play as infants and more aggressive behaviour as adults. Rodents, too, show a similar pattern of adult aggressiveness. In fact, in almost all mammals the male is more aggressive than the female, which has led to the view that we should see aggression in ethological terms.

Ethologists observe animal behaviour in natural settings. Konrad Lorenz, the well-known ethologist, believes that aggression is a natural, spontaneous fighting instinct in both humans and animals, and is directed against members of the same species. However, far from being spontaneous, aggressive behaviour seems to be evoked by specific situations. These situations may be different for males and females. In a large Canadian survey of circumstances in which adults said they became aggressive (see Nicholson, 1979), men gave situations where they had been provoked by another person such as in competitive sport, in relations with the opposite sex or at work. Women, on the other hand, became aggressive when they felt a sense of injustice such as when someone was treated unfairly or there was a matter of principle at stake.

Another difficulty for the ethological view is that situations where we react aggressively are quite rare. We just don't very often become provoked into overt aggression. This has made it rather hard for psychologists to observe and measure aggressive behaviour in the field (i.e. in the 'real world') to test whether men are more aggressive than women. Laboratory evidence suggests that they are, but situations where real aggression can be 'manufactured' in the laboratory are so difficult to arrange that we should be cautious about how far the results can generalize to everyday life. In one experiment (Milgram, 1974), subjects were required to deliver an electric shock every time another 'subject' made an error in a learning task. This second subject was a stooge and no shocks were actually given, although the subjects of the experiment did not know this until afterwards. When presented with a choice of shock intensity, women tended to give much less intense shocks. If the subject was allowed to meet the 'learner' before the experiment, and if the victim could be seen experiencing the painful shocks with phoney moans and groans, women gave even milder shocks when compared to men. Thus, when the situation is arranged so that subjects can feel sympathy for a victim, and guilt and anxiety at their own behaviour, sex differences are most marked. On the other hand, experiments that offer the subjects a good reason for inflicting pain usually show no differences between men and women in their willingness to 'punish' someone.

However, as we said, we have to remain somewhat cautious about these results. Just because men are more willing to inflict unjustified pain on a victim in a laboratory experiment does not mean that they are more aggressive although the accumulation of evidence suggests that they are. A major factor in these studies is conformity or compliance in the presence of an authority figure such as an experimenter. So, is there any evidence of sex differences in conformity or compliance?

Conforming and dependency

It is often said that women are more conforming than men. There is some evidence that this might be true in childhood, but the statement is probably untrue in adulthood. Experimental evidence shows that girls are more obedient to the wishes of adults in childhood (Serbin *et al.*, 1973). Questionnaire studies show that they may also be more conforming in their teens, although such self-reports may merely reflect the stereotype that females are 'supposed' to be more conforming than males. Experimental evidence does not support the self-reports. The most usual experiments again use stooges. Typically, one subject is placed in a room with a number of stooges who all agree with a certain argument, or who all agree, erroneously, on which of two lines that they are shown is longer or which geometric figure has the largest area. Many people suppress their own views or deny the evidence of their own senses and conform to the majority view. Most studies show no differences between the sexes, though some have shown that in the experiments with lines and shapes, women are more likely to agree when challenged by the majority.

Dependency, as such, is difficult to measure, mostly because it is difficult to agree on what it means. Studies of 'proximity-seeking' in children get close to it, since they measure the extent to which the children touch and keep close to adults. If the experiment is long enough, then the results indicate that girls of nursery-school age show greater proximity-seeking to a nurturant adult such as a parent or teacher. Even at age 7, girls spend a larger proportion of their time at home and in the vicinity of parents, which probably reflects the concerns of parents about sexual molesting of girls. Whether women show greater dependency than men is very much an open question. At the moment, there is hardly any evidence that they do.

The bases of sex differences

Now that we have looked at certain cognitive and personality differences between the sexes the question that immediately arises is *why*? What accounts for these differences? You might by now have guessed that the answer revolves around our old friend the nature–nurture problem. In the area of sex differences, the two camps are often referred to as biological determinants and socialization influences, and the debate itself is called sex-typing, but the essence of the problem is the same as the one we met with IQ. Sex-typing is the process by which an individual comes to acquire the behaviour patterns considered appropriate for one sex but not the other. The socialization agents in this process are those individual and institutional influences such as parents, schools, peers and the media which intentionally or not aid sex-typing. The biological determinants are the obvious physical differences, such as the fact that women bear children, and the role of hormones in the process of sex-typing.

You may also guess that the debate continues and that it is impossible to say precisely how much is contributed by biology and how much by socialization since that depends on which authority you read and find convincing. It also depends on what behaviour you study. The following few paragraphs will serve to give you a flavour of the debate and the evidence cited by each side. Interested readers can consult a review by Singleton (1978) for more detail.

The most powerful evidence for the biological determinants side of the argument is sex differences in aggressive behaviour. Advocates point to the fact that in all mammals, the male is more aggressive than the female, which strongly suggests a biological basis. They point to the evolutionary advantages of this in humans:

> The childbearing and physically weaker sex, in order to survive and procreate, would have to develop habits of avoiding rather than seeking combat, of caring for the babies while the stronger, non-childbearing male would go into a hostile world to forage and fight. (Eysenck, 1973, pp. 202–3)

According to their view, the aggressive behaviour depends on sex hormones. Androgens (male sex hormones) increase aggression and estrogens (female sex hormones) decrease aggression. Thus animal studies show that castration in adult males reduces fighting and injections of androgens restores the behaviour. Similarly, injection of androgens into female animals soon after birth makes them more aggressive.

Critics of this evidence point out that it is suspect to generalize from animal studies to humans. Instead, they can point to some remarkable studies of babies born with ambiguous sex organs. Usually, of course, a newborn child is immediately identified as a boy or girl by the external sex organs, and brought up accordingly. In some rare cases this is not so. A child may be born with ambiguous sex organs, and may be reared in a sex contrary to its true biological sex. Only later may the true sex be established by biochemical tests. A study of nineteen individuals raised contrary to their chromosomal sex showed that in every case the role adopted by the boy or girl, man or woman, was in accordance with the sex assigned at birth and the subsequent rearing, rather than with the chromosomal sex. So, a person with male hormones but raised as a girl will dress and behave like a girl and adopt a female gender role throughout life. Such studies are powerful evidence for the role of ascribed sex and socializing influences on gender identity.

You can see that we are unable to draw any firm conclusions on the causes of sex differences. It seems reasonable to conclude, as we did with IQ, that genetic and hormonal influences may lay a foundation for the differences, but socialization plays an enormous role too. There is no answer to the question 'Is it one *or* the other?' Sex-typed behaviour depends on the complex interaction of both biology and psychology, both on nature and on nurture.

Racial differences

Another group with which psychologists have concerned themselves is race. The vast majority of the work in the field of racial differences concerns the intelligence differences between blacks and whites in the USA. Throughout the enormous amount of work which has been done, one fact consistently reappears, and that is that blacks as a group score 12–15 IQ points below whites. This is a large difference and represents about one standard deviation. The facts are not in dispute. What is of concern to researchers in this field, and to us in this chapter, is how these differences can be accounted for – why the difference in intelligence? Some say that it is the obvious result of centuries of prejudice, hostility, segregation and discrimination against the blacks of the USA by the white majority, and of their present inferior social status. Others say that present-day social and economic differences between blacks and whites just do not account for such large differences in IQ score and that the only possible explanation is genetic. In short, blacks are genetically inferior. Still others point to the fact that the differences are IQ not intelligence differences. IQ is not a measure of intelligence, they say, and so the question of why there is a difference in intelligence is meaningless.

We will not concern ourselves too much with this last argument, since that was covered in chapter 3. Before looking in some depth at the first two sets of arguments, though, we need to stand back and look at the debate as a whole.

The debate as a whole

The debate is a particularly difficult one. The difficulty stems from the nature of the subject of race, and the finding of racial differences. The arguments and counter-arguments are often heated, bitter and ideological. On *both* sides of the debate, they are tinged with prejudice or charges of prejudice, racism or charges of racism, smear campaigns or charges of smear campaigns and careful selection of evidence to suit one's case. One has an image of science as a dispassionate, objective process conducted by men and women somehow magically freed from the values, emotions, attitudes and prejudices of ordinary mortals. Science was never really like this. But nowhere is the myth of objective scientific endeavour more vividly exposed than in the race/IQ controversy. It has been argued that it is the duty of psychologists to weigh carefully the evidence presented by the different sides and form their own considered view. Many respond to the intellectual challenge with enthusiasm but find the conclusions extremely difficult to reach. This is because there is no definitive experiment, no seminal series of studies and little by which to judge the mass of good studies on both sides. Others of a more tender-minded disposition baulk at the subject, finding it unpalatable. Some argue that the question of why the IQ differences exist need not be asked in the first place. Certainly, you may require a strong stomach for some of the research. This passage, for example, sounds as if it is describing studies of dogs or cattle but in fact it is talking about a system for grading the skin colour of fellow human beings:

> most studies of hybrid populations have utilized estimates of black-white admixture based not on gene frequencies but on estimates of admixture from pedigrees or physical parameters, such as skin color. Judgements of skin color have often been made by the Milton–Bradley color top method, which uses

adjustable amounts of colored papers (red, black, white and yellow) on a top. The top is spun and each of the component colors is adjusted to yield a blend that matches the color of the subject's skin. (Willerman, 1979, p. 445)

Admitting, then, that the arguments are numerous and complex and that the topic is not to everyone's taste, what are the explanations on each side for the IQ difference? There are lots of arguments supported by evidence, of which the following are among the most important.

Blacks' lack of progress

Advocates of the genetic view point out that despite considerable changes over the past twenty years in the social, political and economic status of blacks in the USA, the 15-point difference remains. If a deprived environment is the explanation, why has the gap not narrowed? Also why, despite opportunities for social advancement that exist (supposedly) for everyone in the USA, have the blacks not moved into a more prominent role in American economic and social affairs? Other immigrants and minorities have made advances, why not the blacks? Finally, educational programmes designed to counteract the social disadvantages of the blacks have failed. The best-known programme is called Head Start, but there have been many such schemes in the USA. They aim to enrich the teaching environment for selected deprived children by very small teacher/pupil ratios, counselling sessions, dedicated teachers, and so on, so as to try to improve the IQ or the school performance of deprived children. It is generally accepted that the vast majority of such intensive and expensive programmes have failed to improve significantly these children's long-term performance when compared to that of control groups not receiving the special treatment. Where there have been improvements they are no more than would be allowed for under the genetic model, which after all does not deny that environment plays some role in intelligence. All this is circumstantial evidence that IQ has a large genetic component, and that environmental explanations cannot account for the IQ difference between blacks and whites.

These arguments are countered strongly by environmentalists. They point to a *long* history of disadvantage and prejudice received by American blacks which has prevented them from upward social mobility and which will take longer than just twenty years to overcome. They point to some spectacular successes of special programmes, such as the Milwaukee Project. Here, the experimental group comprised children whose mothers had low IQs and lived in slum areas. Such children usually grow up with low IQs. The children received an 'enriched environment' provided by skilled mother substitutes at a research centre, while the mothers themselves were counselled and trained. After about four years, large gains were recorded by the children, suggesting that IQ improvements of around 30 points are possible. However, critics have said that the children in the experimental group received practice and training in some of the test items which were later used to measure differences between experimental and control group. This might well have accounted for much of the observed improvement. In fact, the work is very much discredited for these reasons. Environmentalists note that projects that concentrate on schooling are doomed to have little impact anyway, since the disadvantages for many blacks start at home from the day a child is born, are firmly entrenched and continue during and after 'enrichment'. Certainly, black–white differences on IQ tests are present before the school years though this says nothing about the cause.

Socio-economic status

Because socio-economic status (SES) differences between blacks and whites are so obvious, and so often cited as the reason for the IQ deficit, many investigators have tried to control for it statistically. Such studies often show that deficit remains even when SES is controlled. Thus Willerman (1979) quotes a study which showed that the proportion of blacks with an IQ below 75 was much higher than for whites, even when parental SES was controlled. And Shuey's (1966) classic work notes that average differences in IQ remain among high-SES groups:

> The consistent and surprisingly large difference of 20.3 IQ points separating the high-status whites and the high-status colored is accentuated by the finding that the mean of the latter group is *2.6 points below* that of the low-status whites. (Shuey, 1966, pp. 519–20)

Similarly, evidence provided by Jensen shows that SES may be an unimportant cause of the IQ decrement. He compared white, black and Mexican-American children on IQ tests. Blacks had higher SES than Mexican children but lower scores on both verbal and non-verbal (culture-fair) tests. Mexicans did less well on verbal measures, suggesting cultural deprivation. Blacks, on the other hand, did better on verbal tests. This is a fairly common finding. It has been said that blacks do less well on IQ tests because of language difficulties, but in fact they do *better* on these sorts of tests and worse on the so-called culture-fair, non-verbal tests. This has been interpreted as meaning that the IQ decrement is, at least in part, genetic rather than due to lack of familiarity with English or cultural deprivation.

For their part, environmentalists can point to some interesting studies to support their case with SES controlled by a 'natural experiment' rather than statistically. One study by Eyferth (1961) compared the illegitimate children of German mothers and black or white servicemen stationed in Germany after the Second World War. All the German mothers were white and of roughly equal SES. If blacks have 'inferior genes' for intelligence, we would expect the offspring of the black fathers to have lower IQs. No such differences were found. Of course, there is no knowing whether the servicemen were representative of blacks and whites in general, and so no firm conclusions can be drawn. But the results do not support the genetic case.

Another study (Willerman *et al.*, 1974) compared the IQs of children born to white mothers and black fathers with those born to black mothers and white fathers. Genetic explanations would be supported if there were no mean differences between the two groups, since each child has one white and one black parent. If environment is important, then we would expect the children with black mothers to have lower average IQs, since the mother is the main socializing influence in early childhood. Large mean differences were reported in favour of the children with white mothers, which suggests that environmental influences play a large part in the IQ decrement. Similarly, studies of black children adopted by white parents have shown that IQ scores are considerably influenced by rearing conditions. Scarr and Weinberg (1976) showed that when black children, whose natural parents were educationally average, were adopted by advantaged white families, they scored above the IQ and school achievement average of the *white* population.

One explanation for the test differences is that black children are put off doing well because the testers are white. White testers represent authority and white power. Black children are alienated by this and do not do as well as they could.

The evidence does not strongly support this explanation. Some studies using black testers have found that black children performed better than they do with white testers, but most studies find no difference. On balance, the race of the tester does not seem to affect IQ test performance.

Similarly, it has been suggested that blacks are at a disadvantage linguistically. It is not so much that they have poor English but that they speak *black* English. Although it may sound much like English it is very different, with a grammar and structure all its own. IQ tests are written in white English. However, as mentioned above, blacks do not seem to do worse on verbal tests based on standard English than they do on non-verbal tests. Also, when the Stanford-Binet test was rewritten in black English and black testers administered the tests, the IQ decrement remained.

One of the more plausible explanations for the difference is a more general cultural/motivational one: the sub-culture of many blacks is quite different from that of whites. Specifically, it places far less emphasis on the sort of achievement measured by academic success. This feeds through into IQ-test performance as blacks do not see doing well on tests as being as important as do white children. Their culture has taught them to value different things. Since they are not as highly motivated, their average performance is less. Experimental studies do not support this explanation, but are sometimes less than convincing in design. Attempting to raise motivation by payment, for example, had no effect on raising average IQ scores. This is hardly surprising. It is doubtful whether a small financial incentive is enough to overcome a cultural predisposition.

Conclusions

What can we conclude from all this evidence? Perhaps all we can say is that one cannot conclude anything definite. The differences in score between blacks and white are compatible with a genetic interpretation. They are also compatible with a non-genetic interpretation. You must choose whichever view you find most compelling. Whether you are attracted to the genetic or the environmental camp, you can find evidence from the progress or otherwise of blacks, studies of SES, studies of cultural bias and many other sources to support your view.

Since the differences exist, and since IQ is known to correlate with the sorts of thought processes that are useful in our society, perhaps we should concentrate more on studying the complex interaction between genes and environment which helps some and hinders others to do well on tests. That way, we could move nearer to helping everyone to do as well as possible in a society which values the abilities measured by IQ tests. At the moment, a rich, stimulating and varied home and educational environment is more often enjoyed by whites and high-SES groups than blacks and low-SES groups. So the fortunate develop their intelligence towards the top of the range permitted by their genotype (i.e. hereditary component of intelligence). Those from deprived and disadvantaged groups may well develop towards the bottom of their genotype range. Not that we are here aiming to avoid the nature–nurture debate. The hypothesis that people have a range within which they can develop does not assume that there are necessarily any differences in the genetic component of intelligence between different races. Nor does it say that one component is more important than the other. It merely assumes that both heredity and environment play some part in intelligence and encourages us to develop more sophisticated studies of the social, educational and child-rearing practices which might close the IQ gap.

Age differences

When we turn to examine the work of psychologists on the changes that take place with age, we find that the majority of the work has been on intelligence, as is the case with race differences. There has also been a smaller amount of work on the relationship of personality to age, which we will review later in this section. Interested readers can find detailed accounts of age differences in Birren and Schaie (1977).

Intelligence obviously develops with age up to young adulthood. Tasks performed by a child 1 year old would usually be impossible for a baby of 6 months. A child of 3 may have a good conception of number but not the complex mathematical abilities of a child of 13. Binet's early work on the concept of IQ, and Piaget's work on stages of development, are firmly based on the notion of increasing ability with age. But what about later years? Does intelligence go on increasing after the age of, say, 18, does it level off, or does it decline? If it declines, at what age does this process start? These are questions which have been examined by psychologists. The answers, as you will see, are not clear-cut since they depend on the ability and test that you choose. Verbal ability, for example, shows very little decline. Numerical skills and speed of response more often show losses with age. But before we look in more detail at these findings, we need to describe the methods used in the research, since they, too, determine the results of the studies.

Research methods

There are two main approaches to the study of age differences, cross-sectional studies and longitudinal studies. In cross-sectional research, tests are given at the same time to people of different ages, and the results for, say, a 20-year-old group are compared with scores for a 60-year-old group. There are problems with this method since it confounds age with generation (see Davies and Shackleton, 1975). Thus people aged 60 are not just older than 20-year-olds but were born and bred in a different era. Differences between the two age groups, such as less numerical ability in the older group, might be because of a decline in ability or it might be because of a shorter and less stimulating education, a change in teaching methods, a more restricted home environment (with fewer books and no television, for example) or many other causes associated with belonging to a different generation.

Because of deficiencies in cross-sectional research, later studies are more often of the longitudinal type. Here, the same individuals are followed up over a long period of time. So they may be tested at ages 20, 40 and 60 to detect changes. This avoids confounding age with generation. Yet here, too, there are problems. The major difficulty is that it is impossible to study the *same* group over a long period. People die, move away, become untraceable or lose interest in participating in the research. The process is known as selective drop-out. If one starts with a representative sample and the attrition were random, a smaller but still representative sample might remain and all would be well. However, the remaining sample is often not representative, since those of higher SES and above-average abilities tend to remain in the group. An example quoted by Botwinick (1977) illustrates the point. One study tested 500 subjects in 1956. At two subsequent testings, the original 500 had gone down to 302 by 1963 and 161 by 1970. The test scores of the subjects of 1963 and 1970 were examined not only for each of those years, but the *same subjects'* scores at the previous testing dates were examined. At each of these dates, the scores for the remaining subjects were higher than those of the total group. This was the case for each of the five mental abilities tested. At each of the two subsequent testing dates, then, the more able subjects tended to remain in the sample. So sampling bias tends to increase as the study continues. There are a number of possible reasons for selective drop-out. There is evidence (Kleemeier, 1962) that the less able, or those that have declined in ability, tend to die sooner than the others, and so are obviously not available for testing. General ill health and reluctance to put oneself through testing when one is aware of declining abilities may be other reasons.

In summary, the method chosen can affect the findings. The cross-sectional method may magnify or even invent a decline in cognitive ability with age, while the longitudinal method may minimize it. A new method, known as sequential analysis, combines cross-sectional and longitudinal research and opens up new possibilities, but is relatively rarely used as yet.

Ageing and abilities

Figure 8 shows a curve of efficiency quotients (not corrected for age) for the Wechsler Adult Intelligence Scale (WAIS) from cross-sectional studies. It shows a growth of intelligence up to the ages of about 20 to 25 and a regular decline from then on. This curve represents average results from a number of tests and conceals the fact that some sub-tests show steep declines, while others show little or no decline. Tests which are timed, for example, show steep declines with age, while vocabulary tests show little if any decline. Fluid abilities, such as perceptual tasks and abstract intellectual abilities such as the Block Design on the WAIS (where a subject is shown a pattern and must make a copy in wooden blocks) show steeper declines with age than crystallized abilities such as vocabulary and information. However, these cross-sectional studies may be over-pessimistic. Longitudinal studies have shown that vocabulary *increases* up to 50 or 60 years of age, and even spatial- and reasoning-test scores increase up to around age 40. Some writers have argued that decline in mental

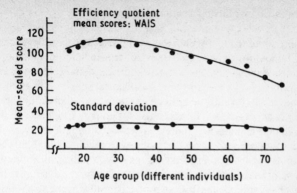

Figure 8 Curve of WAIS efficiency quotient mean scores with age. (After Matarazzo, 1972)

abilities is a myth; there is no good evidence for any major deterioration. Others have suggested that there are declines, but only because older people and their friends and relations expect it to happen, or because of life-style changes with ageing, bereavement and retirement.

On balance, it seems as if a decline in mental ability with age does occur, but it is smaller in magnitude, includes fewer abilities and may begin later in life than earlier, cross-sectional research led us to believe. Experimental work shows that older people are less good at organizing and seeing connections between information when the information is new to them. So problem-solving with unfamiliar material is less efficient. It is important to stress that there may be large individual differences. Such declines as occur do not necessarily occur for everyone or for all abilities. Some retain their abilities longer, perhaps because of genetic differences, more positive attitudes towards abilities and ageing, higher abilities earlier in life and a favourable environment. But as yet we cannot be sure why there are these individual differences. Future research may help us to understand more fully why some people's abilities show a decline and others remain stable, why abilities decline at different rates and whether it is possible to reduce the rate of decline.

There are few studies of changes in children's personality with age since behaviours change so rapidly with development, and the meaning of these behaviours changes. Frequent crying or temper tantrums are common and normal in young children, but are rare and suggest instability in college students. So what studies there are have concentrated on personality changes in adults. A large cross-sectional study (Swenson *et al.*, 1973) showed that hypochondriasis (reporting lots of physical complaints) and feelings of depression increased till ages 40–50 and then levelled off and even declined slightly. Older people also seemed to be less impulsive, agitated, fearful, distractable and worried about themselves. But remember that this is cross-sectional research, and so generation and age variables are confounded. Longitudinal research suggests that some if not all these are generational not ageing differences, since teenagers in 1969 were much less well adjusted (so *more* worried and fearful) than teenagers in 1944 (Woodruff and Birren, 1972). It seems that people feel more stress and strain now than a generation ago.

Personality and adjustment as measured by personality inventories do not seem to change much as we get older. Interests are also remarkably resistant to change. Occupational interests on the Strong Vocational Interest Blank (see chapter 6) are fairly consistent over as much as twenty-two years (Strong, 1951). Yet studies have shown that there are a number of personality, self-concept, interest and value changes with age that are not readily picked up by objective inventories. One important cluster of changes has been called 'disengagement'. It refers to the increased passivity, inner-directedness and withdrawal of the individual from the outer world of people and activities. Obviously, though, this is more characteristic of old people (after retirement, for example) than in middle-aged people. It may well reflect society's expectations of how old people should behave and there is some evidence that disengagement is positively correlated with satisfaction with life.

Finally, it is often said that the old are more conservative than the young. This is true in one sense. Cross-sectional research shows increasing conservatism with age. But you would be very wrong to assume that people *grow* more conservative as they get older. Longitudinal research shows that young people now are less conservative than young people were thirty years ago. Older people are more conservative, but the difference is again due to generation not age.

Conclusion

In chapter 1 we pointed out that everyone is both unique and yet, in certain respects, like a lot of other people. These similar other people are the members of the groups to which we all belong, such as our age group, our sex and our race. One problem of thinking of individuals as members of groups is that it is easy to go on from that to thinking of some groups as superior or inferior to others. In other words, groups can be stereotyped. Most people abhor the negative stereotypes embodied in racism, sexism and (a new term) ageism. But in order to move towards a fuller appreciation of the worth of each individual we need to acknowledge any real differences between groups. We need to establish what those differences are, how they arise and which have practical importance. This is what we have tried to do, in a brief way, in this chapter. Only then we can understand the meaning of the differences and, if necessary, apply our knowledge and techniques to eliminate any ill effects of the differences. Some examples of the practical applications of individual difference theories and techniques is the specific concern of the final chapter.

9 Applications of theory and technique in the field of individual differences

During the course of this book we have referred directly and indirectly to the applications of the specific theories and techniques mentioned. In this final chapter we will look at the application of differential psychology in a more general way. The question to be answered is: To what extent does the study of individual differences enable us to understand and predict the behaviour and performance of people in real-life settings? In trying to find out, the evidence will be examined under a number of headings, namely work behaviour and assessment, occupational choice, and psychological and physical disorders. There are of course many other areas one could look at in this way (academic performance, for example), but it seems more sensible to concentrate on a restricted number of topics in some depth. It is hoped they will serve as illustrations of the broader picture.

Work behaviour and assessment

Intelligence and specific abilities

The use of intelligence measures in selection for work of various kinds goes back to the US army's Alpha test in the First World War.

It is in the field of selection and assessment more than any other that psychologists have had their influence in the world of work, and much of this has revolved round the use of ability measures. How effective have such techniques been? Ghiselli (1966, 1973) collected together data from most of the published studies, using five different types of test: tests of intellectual abilities, of spatial and mechanical aptitude, of perceptual accuracy and of motor abilities, and personality measures. The validity of these kinds of tests in predicting success in training and proficiency in the job was examined for a wide range of occupations. The average validity coefficients are given in figure 9 (for the sake of convenience, the personality-measure data are included in this figure, though we will not discuss them until the next section). There is clearly quite a bit of variability in these findings. Some types of test are better at predicting performance in certain occupations than are others; yet for some jobs all the tests seem quite similar in their effectiveness. Overall, the validity of predictions is very acceptable but not exactly cause for rejoicing. The figures given by Ghiselli relate to single tests being used to predict specific outcomes. As often as not, tests are used in combination, as a test battery. There are various ways of doing this. For example, using the multiple cut-off method, applicants are given one test at a time, and eliminated if they do not attain some pre-set score. This process is carried out for several tests in succession, and so only those candidates who pass all of them remain at the end. Generally, this considerably increases the predictive validity of tests, as is illustrated in a study by Bemis (1968). In this, the average validity for tests individually was 0.22, while for the full battery it was 0.42, using training success as a criterion.

For various technical reasons, not least the small sample sizes used in some of the studies, the Ghiselli findings may rather underestimate the validity of tests. You may at this point be saying to yourself, 'All this talk of validity coefficients is fine, but what does it mean in more concrete terms?' We can try to illustrate it more clearly by looking first at the consequences of not using tests and then considering the productivity and financial implications of using ability tests in selection.

The use of tests by industry in the USA underwent a sharp decline under the impact of equal opportunities legislation. Tests which produced 'adverse impact', that is that gave lower scores for minority-group members and thus reduced the chances of their being selected, were judged illegal. Even without actual prosecu-

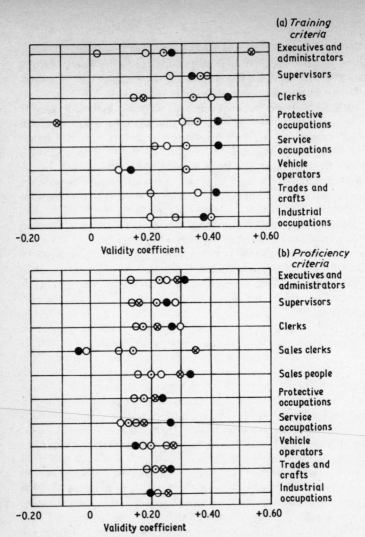

(a) *Training criteria*

Executives and administrators
Supervisors
Clerks
Protective occupations
Service occupations
Vehicle operators
Trades and crafts
Industrial occupations

-0.20   0   +0.20   +0.40   +0.60
Validity coefficient

(b) *Proficiency criteria*

Executives and administrators
Supervisors
Clerks
Sales clerks
Sales people
Protective occupations
Service occupations
Vehicle operators
Trades and crafts
Industrial occupations

-0.20   0   +0.20   +0.40   +0.60
Validity coefficient

● Intellectual abilities ○ Perceptual accuracy ⊗ Personality traits
⊙ Spatial and mechanical abilities ⊖ Motor abilities

Figure 9 Average validity coefficients for five types of psychological test when used in assessing people for jobs in various occupational categories. The top section of the figure (a) shows the validities achieved when performance in training was used as the criterion while the lower section (b) gives the results when job-proficiency criteria were employed. (After Ghiselli, 1966)

tions, many organizations changed their policy on the use of tests. The General Electric Company, responding to US government pressure, dropped the use of job-aptitude tests in selection during the early 1970s. Seven or eight years later, a number of the company's plants found that when they had vacancies to fill through internal promotion, a high percentage of the people they had taken on since dropping the tests were just not promotable. Another example of changing test policy to accommodate the new legislative requirements is provided by US Steel. They had a practice of selecting applicants for skilled-trades apprentice programmes using a battery of cognitive-ability tests. Only the top-scoring proportion of applicants were taken on. Under the changed policy, they drastically reduced the acceptable test-performance level to a minimum standard and went more on the age and experience of the applicant. Data from the apprentice training centre show the results of this change:

1 The scores on competence tests given during training went down significantly.
2 The failure and drop-out rates increased dramatically.
3 For those who did complete the training programme, the time and cost of training increased substantially.
4 The average ratings on later job performance declined.

Both the above examples are cited by Schmidt and Hunter (1981), who go so far as to suggest that the lowered selection standards in the USA may have contributed to that country's much reduced growth rate in productivity. Using new and complex statistical techniques, they convincingly demonstrate that using tests can increase productivity and save costs. For example, using an aptitude test rather than an invalid procedure in the selection of just over 600 computer programmers leads to an estimated productivity improvement of $68 million (at 1981 values) over a ten-year period, providing the top 30 per cent of applicants are accepted. Though the basis for such calculations is beyond the scope of this book, what can be said is that they are certainly not unreasonable or fanciful in their rationale. Even quite modest validity levels potentially lead to major cost-effectiveness benefits. Schmidt and Hunter also point out ways of using tests that are not unfair to minorities and which still achieve almost their maximum predictive value.

While talking about ability tests in this context, it is worth saying something about the relationship between intelligence and managerial performance. It does not seem to be the case that the higher the intelligence-test scores, the better the manager. The relationship seems to be curvilinear (Ghiselli, 1963; Kraut, 1969), meaning that in general, as intelligence-test scores rise, so does management effectiveness – up to a point. Beyond an optimum level of intelligence, as the latter increases, managerial effectiveness begins to decline. So neither very high nor low levels of intelligence are what we want from prospective managers. Gill (1982) looked at the effects of performance feedback and training on students' performance of a managerial simulation task. He found that whilst intelligence did not correlate with performance overall, it *did* correlate with the amount of performance improvement the subjects showed on the task following training. Gill thus suggests that intelligence may be over-emphasized in importance as far as higher-level management performance is concerned, and that the real significance of intelligence is what it tells you about the individual's ability to learn rather than his potential level of achievement (which depends on a lot of other attributes apart from intelligence).

One question that is sometimes raised is why intelligence tests are used in selection when there are, in many cases, academic results from examinations to base an assessment on. This is given further point by the fact that such tests correlate quite highly with academic achievement. One answer is that tests often give another chance to people who did not do well at school for one reason or another. It is not uncommon to find individuals whose scores on ability tests are far higher than one might expect from their examination results. Where this occurs, one has good reason for believing that the individual's potential is greater than the educational record suggests. In this way, ability tests act as a doublecheck. But there is another reason for using intelligence tests alongside, and in some circumstances even in preference to, educational qualifications. Often, they seem to be more sensitive indicators of ability. An example of the superiority of tests is provided by Dulewicz and Fletcher (1982) in a study of an assessment centre for identifying management potential. They found that while intelligence and educational levels of eighty-one managers assessed correlated (0.43), educational levels alone did not correlate with the ratings of potential but intelligence-test results on their own did (0.30).

First, let us take a look at the use made of personality theories and measures in relation to selection. One might reasonably suggest that if the underlying theories have any merit, then the personality measures based on them should be of some relevance in selecting people for jobs. This could be tested out either by correlating scores with job success or by comparing the personality profiles for different occupational groups; the latter should show some differences unless one believes that all personalities are equally efficacious in all jobs. Cattell has provided the most evidence in this area (Cattell *et al*, 1970). Unfortunately, there is not much evidence on the relationship between personality scores on the 16PF Questionnaire and job success, though establishing the criteria of what constitutes job success presents something of a problem. Cattell (1965) quotes the example of a study on bakery salesmen, using as a criterion the amount of the product regularly sold. Salesmen are often a favourite target for research in occupational psychology, not least because they provide such a nice quantifiable criterion in the shape of sales volume. Cattell reports that the effective salesmen tended to be high on the 16PF factors of cyclothymia, surgency and ego strength, or in plainer language they were warm, talkative and emotionally stable and resilient. As Cattell says, this makes sense in terms of most people's experience of salesmen. However, not only is there a dearth of such evidence, but what little there is suffers in many cases from small sample sizes that make its value dubious.

The other kind of study, comparing profiles for different occupational groups, is much more plentiful, again thanks chiefly to Cattell. There are marked differences between such groups on the 16PF Questionnaire. For example, we find that the following groups are characterized by, amongst others, the listed traits, that is they score appreciably differently from the general population on them (the letters in parenthesis indicate 16PF factors – see table 3, p. 55):

Artists		*Clergymen*	
(A)	Reserved	(Q1)	Conservative
(B)	Abstract-thinking	(N)	Forthright
(I)	Tender-minded	(O)	Self-assured
(O)	Apprehensive	(I)	Tender-minded
(M)	Imaginative	(C)	Emotionally stable

Pilots		Physicists	
(G)	Conscientious	(A)	Reserved
(Q3)	Controlled	(B)	Abstract-thinking
(O)	Self-assured	(G)	Expedient
(Q4)	Relaxed	(O)	Self-assured
(L)	Trusting	(Q3)	Controlled

These findings make sense intuitively, which is always comforting. However, the differences in scores between groups are often not of a sufficient magnitude to make them usable in selection. And again, often the sizes of the groups tested are too small to promote great confidence in the data.

So far, we have considered the correlation of personality traits with effectiveness, and profile differences between work groups. It might be inferred that the profile that is typical of a particular occupational group is the one that would be most associated with effectiveness in that kind of work. This is not necessarily the case, as can be seen in the case of scientific researchers. As a group, they are characterized by tender-mindedness or emotional sensitivity (amongst other traits). While this tells us about what is typical of a number of people who have *adjusted* to this occupational role – they have been in the job for some time, which may itself have influenced their personalities – it does not tell us about the factors differentiating between the best and worst of them. In fact, when one looks at the correlation with indices of effectiveness, like the number of research publications a scientist has, it turns out that high effectiveness is associated with *tough*-mindedness. The point is that while personality profiles of occupational groups might eventually prove useful in vocational guidance and perhaps in selection, in that they give us a picture of the type of person who seems likely to adjust quickly to a particular role, they do not tell us who will be the most effective or productive. Rightly or wrongly, it is often the latter that recruiters are looking for.

Cattell's work is of course not the only personality research relevant to selection, but it is probably the broadest and most coherent body of findings. Eysenck's work has had less impact in this direction, though we shall see below that it has other applications in the field of work behaviour. In one investigation of relevance, Eysenck (1967) reports that a survey of 1500 managers found them to be more extraverted and less neurotic than the average population scores on E and N. However, there were quite wide variations within the group. As one might expect, sales and personnel managers were the most extraverted, and consultants and research and development staff the least. A broadly similar pattern, above-average E and below-average N, has been found to characterize successful military pilots in Britain and Japan (Bartram and Dale, 1982).

The potential value of personality measures in selection is one thing; their actual practical value is another. In the studies by Ghiselli that were cited earlier, most of the personality measures used produced predictive validity coefficients of around 0.3 to 0.4, and by and large were not as predictive as intellectual measures for higher-level jobs. These findings cover a wide range of personality measures, many of which were not related to any specific theory of personality in the way that Cattell's and Eysenck's are. All that was said about the Ghiselli data earlier, in relation to intellectual and ability tests, is applicable here; tests used in batteries might improve the prediction, and there are some technical reasons for thinking that the validities may be higher than those indicated by Ghiselli. But there is another factor which is a particular problem in using personality measures in selection, and that is the possibility of candidates faking their responses.

We touched on the topic of faking on personality measures in discussing psychological testing. You may well find that a test correlates with work behaviour or effectiveness when given as part of a research study, but giving it as part of a selection procedure is a different matter. That is the implication of Heron's (1956) finding that applicants for the job of bus driver appeared less neurotic on a personality questionnaire than another group of applicants who completed the questionnaire after the selection process 'for research'. Not all studies support the view that faking is likely. Schwab and Packard (1973) gave personality inventories to two groups of female applicants for jobs in an electrical-manufacturing company. One group of applicants was given the tests as the final part in the selection process, and the other group of applicants took them after they had already been told that they had all been hired. Mean-scale scores did not differ significantly between these groups. None the less, it must be said that the bulk of the evidence seems to run in the contrary direction.

Overall, it would seem that while the use of personality measures are promising in selection, they must be used with great caution at the present time – though, having said that, the most widely used assessment device, the interview, is probably less effective and is used without any caution whatsoever! Moving on from purely selection considerations, what other uses do personality theory and measurement have for helping us understand work behaviour? Let us look at just a few examples.

Eysenck's theory, suggesting as it does differences between introverts and extraverts in arousal levels, conditionability and behaviour, lends itself to a variety of predictions about how people will function at work. Very much in line with the theory, it has been found that extraverts: lack persistence in repetitive tasks (Wilson *et al.*, 1972); have shorter job tenure and more unauthorized absences from work than do introverts (Cooper and Payne, 1967); do not stay in military service as long as intended (Barrett *et al.*, 1975); show more deterioration in performance on monotonous tasks, such as watching sonar or radar screens for infrequent signals, than do introverts (Bakan *et al.*, 1963); and do not perform as well as introverts in the early stages of training on a keypunching job (Savage and Stewart, 1972).

A study by Sterns *et al.* (1983) looked at the relationship between extraversion and job satisfaction. Going on the theory's assumption that extraverts are more 'stimulus-hungry' than introverts (because of their lower levels of cortical arousal), the researchers hypothesized that extraverts would prefer jobs with variety, complexity and cognitive involvement and that they would be less satisfied with clerical work. The results of their study of American civil service clerical staff confirmed these predictions.

The narrow-band personality theories described in chapter 5 have also been much used in work-setting investigations. Locus of control (the degree of internality or externality of the individual) has been employed by Thornton (1978) in a study of career planning. Following up the results of a career-planning workshop for secretaries four months later, he found that secretaries high on internality had taken more action as a consequence of the workshop (exploring potential career goals and finding out how to go about achieving them). Perhaps it is not surprising that internals tend to earn more money, hold higher-status jobs and advance their careers more quickly than do externals (Andrisani and Nestel, 1976). This seems to be a cross-cultural phenomenon too. Pandey and Tewary (1979) report that amongst a group of people applying for money and other support to start up their own businesses in India, individuals with higher levels of internality were more likely to be successful in their application. One might well imagine that the locus of control of managers conducting job interviews or assessing their subordinates' work performance could be a substantial influence in the way they interpret the information they receive and the judgements they make.

Finally, this particular dimension has been related to work stress. External individuals would be likely to see the environment as threatening – they have no control over it, they believe – and would thus be more likely to experience stress. This was confirmed by Kyriacou and Sutcliffe (1979) in a study of 130 school teachers; higher externality was significantly correlated (0.36) with self-reported work stress.

A motivational concept of particular relevance to work performance is need for achievement (nAch). Amongst other things, people high on nAch have been found to stay in jobs longer, to respond better to criticism by improving performance, to choose higher-status careers and to be more successful in gaining promotion.

McClelland and Winter (1969) describe a number of studies reporting positive correlations between nAch scores and various indices of entrepreneurial success, such as increase in size of work force (a sign of the times perhaps; in the 1980s a sign of success is too often a reduction in the work force) or an increase in investment. The motion is that high nAch has a direct influence on the success of the company. However, it seems unwise to assume that high nAch necessarily leads to good management – often it is found in poor managers. High-nAch individuals frequently want to keep a tight hold on the reins themselves, to do everything themselves. And they want clear, short-term, positive feedback – something notoriously absent in many managerial jobs in large organizations. These characteristics do not always make high nAch people particularly easy to work with or to integrate into a team. They are probably better in the role of entrepreneur, setting up stall for themselves. This perhaps implies that nAch is a characteristic developed through childhood experience. However, it may be that the highly competitive climate in some organizations boosts the nAch which was not previously prominent in individuals.

Talking about individual talents as opposed to teamwork brings us to the last example in this brief glimpse of personality study in the work place. If high nAch does not make for a good team person, can we find other personality attributes that do go together and make for effective group performance? On the basis of work by Belbin et al. (1976), the answer seems to be, yes. In studying managers working in groups on management games (simulation

135

exercises), they identified a set of roles or behaviour patterns that were most likely to be present in any team if it were to achieve a high level of performance. They included such roles as 'ideas person' (self-explanatory), 'team worker' (creates and maintains team spirit) and 'monitor evaluator' (analyses proposals and evaluates their worth and feasibility). Belbin and his colleagues found, using a variety of psychological tests including Cattell's 16PF, that they could identify personality characteristics associated with each role. So, by using the test scores, they could establish teams or 'companies' in the management simulations in which the members were complementary in personality and role. This worked so well that a team endowed with only moderate mental and creative ability, but properly balanced in terms of team personalities, performed more effectively and successfully than a more individually talented but less balanced team.

Multiple-assessment procedures

The discussion up to this point has concentrated on the use of psychometric measures of intellect and personality. There are other approaches to assessing individual differences, as was seen in chapter 7. In the Second World War, the British armed forces decided to try to use a variety of procedures together in the assessment of potential officers. The traditional approach to selecting officers (by interviews) seemed to be failing in terms of quantity and quality of those selected. The response was to set up the War Office Selection Board (WOSB), a system whereby candidates were assessed in groups of 8 or 10, taking a series of psychological tests, practical situational exercises (what we referred to as work-sample tests in chapter 7) and being interviewed. This proved most successful. The method was later adopted by the American Office of Strategic Services in selecting secret agents to work behind enemy lines.

The approach of using multiple-assessment techniques with groups of candidates being tested over several days, the process being run by a team of trained assessors, became known as the assessment centre (AC) method. Its first civilian use was by the British civil service shortly after the Second World War. They used it for selecting high-potential administrators and diplomats, and have continued to use the process ever since. Industry was a little slower off the mark, though the Coal Board used assessment-centre techniques in the early 1950s. The real turning-point was the Management Progress Study done in the American Telephone and Telegraph (AT&T) Company in the mid 1950s. Bray and Grant (1966) report the findings of what started out as an investigation of the factors contributing to success or failure in the career development of young managers. The first stage in this was to put the subjects through an intensive assessment procedure using the techniques that have become recognized elements of ACs. They needed this as base-line data from which they could chart changes and look at individual differences. Having collected the data, they locked them away for some four years (this was a longitudinal study). When they looked again at the data they found that the assessments predicted management success (in terms of level attained in the organization) very well. From then on, the method spread quickly as a means of identifying management potential, and today more than 2000 American companies use it. Strangely, but typically, Britain has been slower to take up the application of its own pioneering work on any wide scale, but ACs are now becoming more popular in Britain too.

For a fuller description of the AC method, the reader is referred to Fletcher (1982). Our first concern here is with the light thrown on the effectiveness of different approaches to assessment when they are used together. Table 4 gives the correlations reported by Vernon (1953) between various elements of the AC used by the civil service and the assessments given of job performance between 18 months and 2 years later. Two of the main conclusions to be drawn from those data are that the validity rises with the addition of successive procedures, and that the addition of interviews does not make for a substantial improvement in prediction

Table 4 Cumulative[a] validity of various elements of an assessment centre used in civil service selection. (Vernon, 1953, p. 29)

(1) Entrance exams or verbal intelligence tests	0.22
(2) Ratings of group-discussion exercise	0.32
(3) Ratings of other exercises as well as (2)	0.44
(4) Consideration of (1)–(3) plus two individual interviews	0.47
(5) Consideration of all exercise and interview information and discussion by assessors	0.50
(6) Review of evidence and re-interview of candidates by separate group of assessors	0.58

[a] For example, the correlation coefficient expressed after (3) indicates the validity of the first three modes of assessment taken together.

(though a final re-interview by an *independent* group of assessors does seem to add something useful). Many later studies have produced findings broadly in line with these, in particular the important contribution of the work-sample tests and the beneficial effects of combining the results of different techniques (Huck, 1977). Tests of intellectual ability usually show up as being a useful part of the assessment, but the evidence on personality questionnaires is much less convincing.

The work in ACs has repeatedly supported an earlier finding of some significance in the assessment of individual differences. Meehl (1954) reviewed evidence from studies which compared two types of judgement, clinical and statistical. In the former, assessors combine all the information they have about an individual in their own heads and come out with a prediction; this is what happens in interviews and most other assessment situations. The statistical approach, on the other hand, combines all the information together in an appropriate statistical operation. This involves not only the correlation of individual pieces of assessment information with the behaviour to be predicted, but the calculation of the differences in predictiveness of the different bits of information. The statistical approach uses a formula that combines and 'weights' the information (test scores, etc.) according to how strongly correlated each item is with the outcome to be predicted. Meehl found that the statistical approach won hands down over clinical judgement – it consistently gave rise to greater predictive accuracy. Similarly, many investigators (e.g. Wollowick and McNamara, 1969) have compared the correlation between the judgements of the assessors running an AC and the criteria used (salary progression, performance ratings, promotions, etc.), with the correlation achieved by simply treating the AC scores of the candidates in a statistical fashion. The statistical approach repeatedly comes out on top. It seems that our inadequate information-processing capacities frequently lead us to do less well than we should on the basis of the evidence our assessment devices provide.

The very considerable amount of information provided by several days of tests, interviews and exercises has proved a tempting target for factor analysis. Here we encounter echoes of the debate described in chapter 3 on the existence of *g*. Factor analysis of AC scores or assessors' ratings have in some cases produced a 'general effectiveness' factor (e.g. Bray and Grant, 1966) while in others they have not (e.g. Fletcher and Dulewicz,

1984). As with intelligence-test scores alone, much depends on the factor-analytic technique used.

Finally, the AC technique is increasingly used not just for selection as such, but for helping in the career development of those assessed. Careful feeding back of information on strengths and weaknesses can increase the individual's self-awareness and put him or her in a better position to know what development steps (training courses, job moves, etc.) should be taken.

Individual differences and occupational choice

Occupational choice and counselling is often also referred to as vocational or career choice, but these latter two terms are less satisfactory; 'vocation' implies some kind of 'calling', and occupational choices in many cases do not involve a career as such. There are two main theoretical approaches to the occupational-choice process. The first, historically, was the differentialist viewpoint. This essentially involves an analysis of the job and of the person, using the results to match the two as optimally as possible. Most people's ideas of vocational guidance are consistent with this approach. The implication is that there is one job or set of jobs that an individual is best suited to in terms of personality, ability and interests, and that is what the person should be guided towards. This, however, presents a rather static picture of human beings, and in more recent years a second major viewpoint has emerged, that of the developmentalists. The developmentalists emphasize the processes and stages of occupational choice that go on throughout the whole of life. Occupational choice and counselling, from this point of view, are not a one off event but a continuing and changing process.

Major theories of both kinds have strong connections with general personality theory. For example, the best-known developmental theory, that of Donald Super, tries to bridge the gap between this area of psychology and personality theory by conceptualizing occupational choice as the formulation and implementation of a self-concept. The individual is seen as progressing through a series of stages in which the self-concept grows and changes through interaction with the environment. The person develops an awareness of talents and abilities, of likes and dislikes, and collects information about work. After a good deal of exploration, the vocational self-concept is established, but further changes will take place as a person progresses through different stages of working life right up to retirement.

J.L. Holland's differentialist theory – an updated version of the traditional differentialist approach – is not just linked to personality theory, it is itself a full-blown theory of personality. The basic assumptions underlying it are that people can be categorized into six personality types (realistic, investigative, artistic, social, enter-prising and conventional). There are six types of environment that correspond to these, and people search for the matching environment type as this will permit them to display the abilities, values, etc., associated with their kind of personality. Behaviour at work, says Holland, results from the individual's personality type and its interaction with the characteristics of the environment type. If the notion of just six personality types seems a bit too simple, one should add that Holland works with *patterns* of personality. He produces measures of his types (e.g. the Holland Vocational Preference Inventory) that give an individual's score on each type. By ranking the person's scores in descending order of how strongly he or she fits each type, you end up with a total of 720 possible personality patterns. Holland has produced an 'occu-pation finder' which lists jobs appropriate to the different person-ality patterns (Holland, 1973).

The use of psychological tests in occupational counselling is identified more with the differentialists, but they can be and are used by those taking the developmentalist stance. In the latter case, the counsellor would be particularly keen to avoid any assumption that the test results gave a fixed and permanent picture of the individual. What sort of tests are used in occu-pational counselling, and how are they used? The most frequently employed measures are interest inventories and tests of aptitude. In Britain the most frequently encountered versions of the former are the APU Occupational Interests Guide, Kuder Vocational Preference Record, Holland Vocational Preference Inventory, Strong-Campbell Interest Inventory and Rothwell Miller Interest Blank.

With regard to aptitude tests, the Department of Employment has developed its own. Known as DEVAT (Department of Employ-ment Vocational Aptitude Test), this battery of tests has been widely used by the careers service in Britain and measures mathematical arithmetic, mechanical and verbal abilities, amongst others. Interest tests are used as measures of motivation. The reason for using aptitude tests is obvious. Tests of general intellectual level are sometimes used in this sort of counselling, particularly where suitability for various kinds of academic study is in question, or where for one reason or another there is an absence of other indicators of intellectual level. Personality inventories as such are used less frequently. A little way back we noted the possibility in selection of using Cattell's profiles of 16PF scores for different occupational groups. They could also be used in occupational counselling, and in fact are probably more helpful in this context than in selection. But most of the same problems are relevant here too; the profiles, often based on small samples, only give an indication of average characteristics of people in that job category – they tell you nothing about success or effectiveness in the job, nor do they necessarily show that someone with different personality characteristics would dislike the work. Personality data, when used, have to be treated with the greatest caution.

The general approach to using individual-difference measures in occupational counselling is not perhaps what the layman would expect. There is a great deal of emphasis on sharing the process of interpreting and using the test results with the client. This is part of the general orientation towards counselling rather than 'guidance'. The concepts of Carl Rogers' non-directive therapy have influenced practitioners in this field and the counselling process is seen as one in which clients are helped to make their own decisions, rather than being told what is 'best' for them (Shackleton and Spurgeon, 1982). Thus, the individual's own ideas about the test results are of fundamental importance. The other aspect of test-use here is that it is only one part of the counselling process. The whole exercise does not, and should not, rest on the test information. Such data have to be incorporated with all the other sources of information about the person, and interpreted in the light of that. Probably the greatest mistake that unqualified test-users make is to place too great an emphasis on the tests and to use them in a rather directive, mechanistic fashion.

If the above remarks seem rather to play down the use of psychometric measures, one might wonder what such measures do contribute. Is the counselling process more effective with them than without them? A classic series of studies carried out in Birmingham in the 1930s and 1940s provides some answer. In the first of these (Allen and Smith, 1932), 328 school leavers were divided into control and experimental groups. The former received careers advice from employment officers on the basis of interviews, educational reports, and so on. The experimental group was similarly treated, but here the employment officers had test results available also. Follow-up of the 86 per cent who could be traced two years later showed that 49 per cent of the control group were in jobs consistent with the advice given, compared to 61 per cent of the experimental group. Individuals in the experimental group who had entered work congruent with the guidance given were rated higher on their suitability for their jobs by both themselves and their employers than any of the other groups in the study (i.e. congruent and non-congruent control groups, and the non-congruent experimental group). A second and larger study in 1944 supported these findings and found that the differences between groups grew even larger (92 per cent compared to 47 per cent in congruent jobs) over a longer follow-up period. On the less positive side, Butler *et al.* (1972) found that adding the Kuder Vocational Preference Record to a counselling procedure did not lead to any increase in satisfaction with the guidance received or with subsequent employment. A review of evidence by Shrauger and Osberg (1981) found that self-assessment of likely career or job choice was more accurate than interest measures in predicting what work the individual eventually took. However, there was no evidence as to whether self-assessment methods predicted job success or job satisfaction as well as or better than interest inventories.

Overall, the evidence is probably more in favour of the use of tests in occupational counselling than against, but the case is not yet convincingly established one way or the other. This is because of methodological problems in the studies carried out, mostly in relation to the criteria used for evaluating the effectiveness of counselling interventions. As Watts and Kidd (1978) point out, the greater emphasis on developmental approaches has not been reflected in the research on effectiveness. Apart from anything else, for such research to be carried out there has to be clearer specification of what the appropriate change criteria are for assessing the impact of counselling.

Psychological and physical disorders

Diagnosis and individual differences in psychopathology

One of the great problems that has afflicted the field of abnormal psychology is the lack of a satisfactory diagnostic system. The traditional approach to describing and classifying psychological disorders is based on the medical model. In other words, they are treated much the same as if they were physical disorders; and just as reasonably clear-cut categories are used to describe physical ailment (bronchitis, influenza, gastro-enteritis, and so on), so the psychological disorders were split up into nice, neat categories. Thus, neurotic disorders were broken down into such things as anxiety states, obsessive-compulsive reactions, phobias and hysterical conversion or dissociative reactions. The more serious disorders, the psychoses, were differentiated into organic (having an identifiable physical origin) and functional groups, the latter including such severe problems as schizophrenia and depression for neither of which was there any known physical cause.

The adoption of this kind of approach to describing psychological problems made sense in view of the historical development of work in this field. It had become mainly the province of the medical profession, and as this way of looking at things had worked for physical disorders, why not apply it to mental problems too? The trouble is that while we know quite a lot about the causative agents in illness, we have little such knowledge about psychological abnormalities. And so, not surprisingly, we find that the rather superficial way of describing them does not seem to work very well. Patients stubbornly refuse to show patterns of symptoms in the way the medical text-books talk about them. The schizophrenic individual may show elements of neurotic anxiety and of depression. The anxiety-state neurotic may exhibit signs of compulsiveness and of hysterical tendencies. The traditional categorical approach to describing psychological disorder does not work. Spitzer and Fleiss (1974), reviewing a number of studies in which the diagnoses of different psychiatrists on the same patients had been compared, found that there was an alarmingly high tendency for the clinicians to disagree. In fact the only diagnoses that satisfactory agreement was reached on were organic brain syndrome, alcoholism and mental deficiency!

A great deal of work in the field of individual differences suggests an alternative approach to the way we conceptualize psychological disorders. You will have noticed that most of the personality and intellectual variables mentioned in the course of this book are assumed to be continua. We do not think in terms of some people being extraverted while others are Machiavellian or internal in locus of control (though it is easy to slip into this kind of simplified way of thinking). In all of these cases, the whole population is seen as being represented on a dimension. There is no fundamental cut-off point where you 'cease' to be called an extravert and become an introvert, or where you are switched from being Machiavellian to non-Machiavellian. Many differential psychologists would argue that the same applies to psychological disorders – we should take a dimensional rather than a categorical view. The leading exponent of this approach is Eysenck. As we saw in chapter 5, he believes that neuroticism and psychoticism are two of the main dimensions of personality, and thus that there are only quantitative, not qualitative, differences between people on these variables.

Eysenck's theory not only suggests that we drop the conventional, categorical approach to describing disorders, but also tries to explain how it is that people put into what seem to be similarly stressful circumstances develop different neurotic reactions. For example, the person who is high on neuroticism (N) and high on introversion (I) is characterized by high autonomic reactivity (strong emotional responses) and ready conditionability, according to the theory. Such a person exposed to a noxious stimulus, say a bite from a dog, is much more likely to develop a phobic fear of dogs than is someone who is either low on N (a less fearful response) or low on I (takes more exposures to condition a response). So, Eysenck suggests that 'dysthymic' disorders (neurotic disturbance of mood or emotion) are associated with the high-N/high-I personality. The reason why a person suffers from one type of dysthymic disorder rather than another, for example obsessive-compulsive reaction as opposed to a phobia, is due to situational variables and the individual's conditioning history. On the other hand, an individual who is high on neuroticism and high on *extraversion* (E) is likely to display (given the appropriate stressful circumstances) disorders or deviant behaviour characterized by a failure to adequately learn socially acceptable responses. Examples of these include drug addiction, alcoholism and sexual deviations. The failure of the high-E individual to form conditional responses easily, when linked with high N, thus produces a quite different pattern of psychological abnormality.

Eysenck's attempt at explaining why individual differences occur in psychopathology goes beyond what has been said here, but this description serves to illustrate the approach. His theory seems to work better with regard to predictions about high N and high I than it does for high N and high E. Irrespective of whether the details of his theory are correct, the general notion of a dimensional approach to psychological abnormality is certainly not invalidated.

Most of the other contributions of differential psychologists in this field have been more limited in their area of concern than has Eysenck's comprehensive theory. That, however, does not mean that they have been less valuable. As an example, we might take the work of many psychologists and look at it as one topic – the use of psychometric tests in diagnosis. Very often here the practical benefits of the results achieved outweigh their significance for advances in theory. One particular area where tests have proved their usefulness is in assessing brain damage and deterioration. They may be given to help determine whether changes in the behaviour of an old person reflect the onset of senile dementia; to investigate the possibility of organic causes for a patient's memory loss; to act as a base line for a series of observations, either to see whether a progressive deterioration in performance is taking place or to measure the effects of treatment on mental functioning; and to test certain aspects of behaviour and performance for the purpose of relating them to specific areas of brain damage.

Tests used in this way can often be more sensitive indicators than other means available (though sometimes tests are the only means available), but their application is a highly skilled task. The WAIS is quite widely employed in this context. A high discrepancy between verbal and performance intelligence (e.g. the latter 20 points below the former) for a man aged 30 years might indicate a possibility of organic damage, though the pattern of individual sub-test scores on the WAIS would be important in making such a judgement. This is a fairly simple example, and one has to add that many clinicians use their experience to obtain a lot of information about the patient from the way he or she behaves in the testing session as well as from the test results themselves. Things get more complex when the clinician is faced with the task of identifying or confirming the extent of damage to a particular area of the brain (for example in the case of a motorcycle-crash victim). Careful selection of a number of tests is required, and a series of them will be administered to the patient. For example, if damage to the frontal areas of the brain is suspected, tests assessing the individual's capacity for abstraction, planning, checking programmes of action and verbal behaviour might be appropriate.

Diagnosis of brain damage and deterioration is one thing, but diagnosis in the areas of neurosis and functional psychoses is quite another, as we have seen. Can psychometric tests add anything of value in these less well-defined types of psychological disorder? The overall conclusion is that in most cases, tests (usually personality inventories in this context) may be useful in suggesting lines of enquiry or for checking hypotheses, but their validity is not sufficiently high to make precise diagnosis. However, if tests are usually not good enough for saying which type of disorder a patient is suffering from, the same is also true in lots of cases of psychiatrists' judgements, as we noted earlier. We are back up against the problems of the diagnostic system as a whole.

Therapy

Work on individual differences and their measurement has been used to predict the effects of therapy, to help us in our understanding of the therapeutic relationship and to evaluate the outcome of psychological therapies. To put this in context, however, we need first to sketch in some of the background on therapy. It was Eysenck's (1952b) attack on the effectiveness of psychotherapy which triggered off much of this research. He demonstrated that psychotherapists had failed to establish the superiority of the effects of their approach to treatment over the effects of no treatment at all. In both cases, said Eysenck, about two-thirds of patients get better in time. Since then, a great deal of research has gone into trying to find out just how effective psychotherapy really is. More recently, investigators in this field have realized that such a broad question as 'Does psychotherapy work?' is rather meaningless. What they are trying to find now is the answer to a question more like 'Under what conditions, and with which patients, does therapy work best?' In other words, we need to specify in more detail individual differences in patient and in therapist, as well as taking account of the nature of the therapy, when doing research on effectiveness. This goes not just for psychotherapy but also for behaviour therapy (therapy based on concepts taken from learning theory).

As an example of seeking to predict who will or will not benefit from treatment, a study by Ross *et al.* (1983) will serve. This concentrated on the relationship between the problem of obesity and locus of control.

If the theory of locus of control is right, then internal individuals should respond to treatment more successfully as they should be better able to exercise self-control over their eating behaviour than should externals. The latter would be expected to continue to be controlled by the external, environmental stimuli that maintain their inappropriate eating habits. Ross and his colleagues took locus-of-control measures on 133 obese women before treatment and found that the individual's degree of internality/externality did indeed predict the extent to which she complied with treatment and the amount of weight gain in the six months following treatment. As expected, internals complied more and put less weight on again after treatment had finished.

More generally, greater effects of psychotherapy seem to be associated with patients of higher intelligence (Smith and Glass, 1977), and with patient–therapist similarity. Various aspects of similarity have been looked at, though the results have not all been in the same direction (Gomes-Schwartz et al., 1978). For example, Pettit et al. (1974) found that complementarity rather than similarity of values increased the likelihood of patients from lower socio-economic groups staying in therapy rather than giving up; the aspect of complementarity looked at here was submissiveness to authority (patients high on this matched with therapists low on it). Not surprisingly, sex is another factor that had attracted attention in this context. Is it best to have patient and therapist of the same sex? As usual, there are no simple answers, and the effects of such sex matching depend on a host of other variables such as the patient's early relationship with parents and areas of conflict (Mogul, 1982). No particular personality match between patients and therapists has been discovered as important, as yet. But there are some findings on patient personality and response to different types of treatment. For example, Di Loreto (1971) found that client-centred therapy seemed to work best with introverts while systematic desensitization, a form of behaviour therapy, worked equally well with introverts or extraverts.

One of the main difficulties in evaluating therapy is in the criterion used to measure its effect. All the criteria available have drawbacks. Clinicians' ratings of patient improvement tend to be highly subjective, and the patients' own responses to direct questioning may be distorted and unrealistic if their psychological problems have not been overcome. Psychometric tests have been used as a way round some of these difficulties. An aim that many therapies have is to increase the individual's feelings of control, as the lack of such feelings seems to be a potent factor in many psychological disorders. Levenson (1973) found that during a month of treatment a group of neurotic and psychotic patients significantly increased their belief in internal control on the

Levenson Locus of Control scale. The patients still tended to be more external than average in their beliefs about the wider world, but whether that is irrational is highly arguable.

Personality-test scores are often employed as before-and-after measures of therapeutic effects, but as is generally the case with test results, interpretation has to be treated with great caution. Rosen (1966) gives the example of a patient whose MMPI ego-strength-scale score rose from 34 to 40 after four months of psychotherapy. Just how meaningful is this? Not very, according to Rosen. He found that 19 per cent of patients improved their ego-strength scores by 6 or more points on retesting without receiving any psychotherapy at all. To assess the meaning of a change in test scores, you need to know about the normal degree of test–retest variation in scores for any particular instrument. Even with such knowledge, it would be unwise to rely solely on psychometric-test responses as a guide to patient improvement. Eysenck notes that patients often get stereotyped notions of the way they are supposed to be after treatment and reply accordingly, perhaps trying to please, or at least not disappoint, their therapist. All the other limitations of tests that we discussed in chapter 7 apply here too, but they do have a contribution to make in helping to assess the effects of therapy and will almost certainly continue to be used as one of a number of evaluation criteria.

Individual differences and the prevention of physical illness

Working on the principle that prevention is better than cure, it would be of immense value to society if any individual differences in psychological make-up associated with particular health problems could be identified. Early detection of 'at risk' personality profiles would offer the chance of taking prophylactic measures. There is increasing evidence that some personality attributes are linked to physical illness. Perhaps the best-known of these is the relationship between Type A behaviour and coronary heart disease (see pp. 67–8). There is also reason for believing that there may be a cancer-prone personality as well as coronary-prone one. The cancer-prone person is described as one who represses emotion (but see the findings below), feels unworthy, needs structure and order, tries to carry on normal routines in the face of considerable adversity, and allegedly suffers underlying depression and feelings of despair and hopelessness. The trouble is that, unlike the Type A findings, many of the observations that this idea rests on come from poorly controlled studies, and it is possible that the personality pattern depicted above is an effect of cancer rather than a cause. There are some more convincing studies, fortunately. Sheehan (1977) compared the personalities of women suspected of having breast cancer before a biopsy revealed malignancy or non-malignancy. The group who were subsequently found to have cancer showed higher levels of depression than the non-cancer group and also tended not to expect love, understanding, security or family closeness. A somewhat similar study by Greer and Morris (1975) found that higher breast-cancer rates were associated with the way that anger was handled. Women who very strongly suppressed anger (not expressed it openly more than twice in their adult lives) *or* who were very prone to expressing it (frequent outbursts of temper) were both more likely to be found to be suffering from malignancy.

Other attempts have been made to link personality with illness. But as indicated above, great care has to be taken that one is not just discovering the effects of the malady on the individual's personality. Numerous studies have shown that asthmatics seem to be characterized by such traits as anxiety, sensitivity, perfectionism and obsessionality. The investigations have compared asthmatics to 'normals', but Neuhas (1958) took the process a stage further and included a group of children with cardiac conditions as well as asthmatic and healthy children. Comparing the three groups on personality-test scores, asthmatics were found to be more neurotic than healthy children, but so were the cardiac-group children. It seems likely that the neuroticism is a reaction to chronic illness. There is plenty of other evidence suggesting that prolonged illness has detrimental psychological effects. Sternbach *et al.* (1973) compared groups of acute and chronic low-back-pain sufferers on the MMPI. They found that the chronic patients had very high scores on scales measuring elements of neuroticism (hypochondriasis, depression and hysteria) while the acute patients were significantly lower and within the normal range for such scores. The implication is that the chronic group would probably have produced a normal personality profile in the early stages of their complaint, but the extended experience of pain has left its mark on their personalities.

Studies producing results of this sort may not help us in our understanding of the causes of illness, nor do they assist in identifying high-risk groups and thus aid prevention. But they are interesting and important none the less, as they focus on a much

149

neglected area, the impact of illness on psychological functioning. This is an aspect of medical treatment that is all too often ignored. Yet, as Rachman and Phillips (1978) point out, contemporary medicine has increasingly to deal with chronic disorders and disabilities as the episodic, infectious illnesses are conquered, and it is with these long-term problems that psychological factors are most important. Quite apart from the need to maintain the mental well-being of the individual for its own sake, failure to do so exacerbates health problems and slows recovery. An illustration of the latter is provided by Imboden *et al.* (1961) who found that individuals high on personality-test scores of depression (taken before onset of illness) took longer to recover from influenza.

Another approach to assessing and predicting individual differences in vulnerability to illness is found in the work of Holmes and Rahe (1967). They developed a measure known as the Social Readjustment Rating Scale (SRRS). This is simply a list of life events that require some adaptive or coping behaviour, for example marriage, moving house, trouble with the boss, changing work responsibilities. Each event has been given a score of 'life-change units' (LCUs) according to how much readjustment it is likely to require of an individual (death of spouse carries an LCU score of 100, the highest of all). A person completing the SRRS simply ticks any event that has happened in the past six months or a year. The LCU score is the sum of the individual LCU scores for each event. High scores on the SRRS are associated with increased likelihood of illness. Rahe *et al.* (1970) used the LCU scores based on life events in the previous six months to separate 2500 naval personnel into high-risk and low-risk groups, and found that in the next six months the former group had 90 per cent more illness than the latter. The general notion is, then, that too many life events within a limited period generate high levels of stress, which in turn increases vulnerability to illness. There are a number of methodological problems with the research on life events and illness (Minter and Kimball, 1980), but the evidence is sufficient to warrant paying a good deal of attention to life events. Here, however, we return to the argument between the personality-trait theorists and the 'situationalists' that was discussed in chapter 5. The life-event literature can be seen as the situational side of the equation, whilst the material on Type A behaviour is more in line with the general personality-theory approach. The middle ground of the interactionist point of view again seems most appropriate. One could well imagine, for instance, that the Type A personality generates more life events and thus more stress for himself or herself.

Conclusion

In this final chapter we have tried to give some glimpses – and they can be little more than that – of how the theories and techniques associated with the field of individual differences can be applied to understanding and tackling practical problems. The range of such applications is vast and growing all the time, to the extent that most people in society have come into contact with them in one form or another. There are still many contradictory findings, inadequacies in theory and methodological deficiencies, but sufficient has been achieved already to indicate the great potential of this field of study. We hope that having read this book, you agree with this conclusion.

Suggestions for further reading

Chapter 1

Anastasi, A. (1982) *Psychological Testing*, 5th edn, New York, Macmillan.
Kline, P. (1980) 'The psychometric model', in Chapman, A.J. and Jones, D.M. (eds), *Models of Man*, Leicester, British Psychological Society.
Tyler L.E. (1978) *Individuality*, London, Jossey-Bass.

Chapter 2

Fransella, F. (ed.) (1981) *Personality*, London, Methuen.
Kline, P. (1981) *Fact and Fantasy in Freudian Theory*, 2nd edn, London, Methuen.
Mischel, W. (1981) *Introduction to Personality*, 3rd edn, New York, Holt, Rinehart & Winston.
Storr, A. (ed.) (1983) *Jung: Selected Writings*, London, Fontana.
Willerman, L. (1979) *The Psychology of Individual and Group Differences*, San Francsiso, W.H. Freeman.

Chapter 3

Eysenck, H.J. versus Kamin, L. (1981) *Intelligence: The Battle for the Mind*, London, Pan.
Gould, S.J. (1981) *The Mismeasure of Man*, New York, W.W. Norton.

Pyle, D.W. (1979) *Intelligence: An Introduction*, London, Routledge & Kegan Paul.

Vernon, P.E. (1979) *Intelligence: Heredity and Environment*, San Francisco, W.H. Freeman.

Chapter 4

Barron, F. and Harrington, D.M. (1981) 'Creativity, intelligence and personality', *Annual Review of Psychology*, 32, 439–76.

De Bono, E. (1970) *Lateral Thinking: A Textbook of Creativity*, London, Ward Lock.

Koestler, A. (1964) *The Act of Creation*, London, Hutchinson.

Vernon, P.E (ed.) (1973) *Creativity*, Harmondsworth, Penguin.

Chapter 5

Bannister, D. and Fransella, F. (1971) *Inquiring Man: The Psychology of Personal Constructs*, Harmondsworth, Penguin.

Cattel, R.B. and Kline, P. (1977) *The Scientific Analysis of Personality and Motivation*, London, Academic Press.

Eysenck, H.J. and Eysenck, S.B.G. (1969) *Personality Structure and Measurement*, London, Routledge & Kegan Paul.

Hall, C.S. and Lindzey, G. (1957) *Theories of Personality*, New York, Wiley.

Mischel, W. (1981) *Introduction to Personality*, 3rd edn, New York, Holt, Rinehart & Winston.

Chapter 6

Korman, A.K. (1974) *The Psychology of Motivation*, New Jersey, Prentice-Hall.

London, H. and Exner, J.E. (eds) (1978) *Dimensions of Personality*, New York, Wiley.

Weiner, B. (1980) *Human Motivation*, New York, Holt, Rinehart & Winston.

Chapter 7

Anastasi, A. (1982) *Psychological Testing*, 5th edn, New York, Macmillan.

Cronbach, L.J. (1970) *Essentials of Psychological Testing*, New York, Harper & Row.

Mackenzie Davey, D. and Harris, M. (eds) (1982) *Judging People*, London, McGraw-Hill.

Vernon, P.E. (1964) *Personality Assessment: A Critical Survey*, London, Methuen.

Chapter 8

Eckberg, D.L. (1979) *Intelligence and Race: The Origins and Dimensions of the IQ Controversy*, New York, Praeger.

Marois, M. (ed.) (1981) *Ageing: A Challenge to Science and Society, 3: Behavioural Sciences and Conclusions*, London, Oxford University Press.

Nicholson, J. (1979) *A Question of Sex: The Differences between Men and Women*, London, Fontana.

Willerman, L. (1979) *The Psychology of Individual and Group Differences*, San Francisco, W.H. Freeman.

Chapter 9

Davison, G.C. and Neale, J.M. (1982) *Abnormal Psychology*, 3rd edn, New York, John Wiley.

Muchinsky, P.M. (1983) *Psychology Applied to Work*, Homewood, Illinois, Dorsey Press.

References and name index

The numbers in italics following each entry refer to page numbers in this book.

Abramson, L.Y., Seligman, M.E.P. and Teasdale, J.P. (1978) 'Learned helplessness in humans: critique and reformulation', *Journal of Abnormal Psychology*, 87, 49–74. *65*

Adams-Webber, J. (1979) *Personal Construct Theory: Concepts and Applications*, New York, Wiley. *62*

Allen, E.P. and Smith, P. (1932) *The Value of Vocational Tests as Aids to Choice of Employment*, Birmingham, City of Birmingham Education Committee. *141*

Allport, G. W. (1961) *Pattern and Growth in Personality*, New York, Holt, Rinehart & Winston. *48*

Anastasi, A. (1982) *Psychological Testing*, 5th edn, New York, Macmillan. *89, 97*

Andrisani, P.J. and Nestel, C. (1976) 'Internal–external control as a contributor to and outcome of work experience', *Journal of Applied Psychology*, 61, 156–65. *134*

Arvey, R.D. and Campion, J.E. (1982) 'The employment interview: a summary and review of recent research', *Personnel Psychology*, 35, 281–322. *100*

Atkinson, J.W. (1957) 'Motivational determinants of risk-taking behaviour', *Psychological Review*, 64, 359–72. *78, 79*

Bakan, P., Belton, J.A. and Toth, J.C. (1963) 'Extraversion–introversion and decrement in an auditory vigilance task', in Buckner, D.N. and McGrath, J.J. (eds) *Vigilance: A Symposium*, New York, McGraw-Hill. *134*

Bannister, D. (1966) 'A new theory of personality', in Foss, B. (ed.) *New Horizons in Psychology*, Harmondsworth, Penguin. *13*

Bannister, D. and Fransella, F. (1971) *Inquiring Man: The Psychology of Personal Constructs*, Harmondsworth, Penguin. *60*

Baron, R.A., Byrne, D. and Kantowitz, B.H. (1980) *Psychology: Understanding Behavior*, 2nd edn, Tokyo, Holt-Saunders. *92*

Barrett, G. V., Bass, B.M., O'Connor, E.J., Alexander, R.A., Forbes, J.B. and Cascio, W.F. (1975) *Relationship among Job Structural Attributes, Retention, Aptitude and Work Values*, Technical Report No. 3, Department of Psychology, University of Akron, Ohio. *134*

Barron, F. and Harrington, D.M. (1981) 'Creativity, intelligence and personality', *Annual Review of Psychology*, 32, 439–76. *43*

Bartram, D. and Dale, H.C.A. (1982) 'The Eysenck Personality Inventory as a selection test for military pilots', *Journal of Occupational Psychology*, 55, 287–96. *133*

Bayne, R. (1982) 'Interviewing', in Mackenzie Davey, D. and Harris, M. (eds) *Judging People*, London, McGraw-Hill. *99*

Belbin, R.M., Aston, B.R. and Mottram, R.D. (1976) 'Building effective management teams', *Journal of General Management*, 3, 23–9. *135*

Bem, S.L. (1975) 'Sex role adaptability: one consequence of psychological androgyny, *Journal of Personality and Social Psychology*, 31, 634–43. *15*

Bemis, S.E. (1968) 'Occupational validity of the General Aptitude Test Battery', *Journal of Applied Psychology*, 52, 240–4. *127*

Birren, J. E. and Schaie, K. W. (eds) (1977) *Handbook of the Psychology of Aging*, New York, Van Nostrand-Reinhold. *120*

Bishop, D.V.M. (1977) 'The P scale and psychosis', *Journal of Abnormal Psychology*, 86, 127–34. *53*

Block, J. (1978) 'Claridge and Birchall, different forms of the P scale and dependable moderators', *Journal of Abnormal Psychology*, 87, 669–72. *53*

Botwinick, J. (1977) 'Intellectual abilities', in Birren, J.E. and Schaie, K.W. (eds) *Handbook of the Psychology of Aging*, New York, Van Nostrand-Reinhold, 580–605. *121*

Brand, C.R. and Deary, I.J. (1982) 'Intelligence and inspection time', in Eysenck, H.J. (ed.) *A Model for Intelligence*, New York, Springer. *28*

Bray, D.W. and Grant, D.L. (1966) 'The assessment centre in the measurement of potential for business management', *Psychological Monographs*, 80 (625), whole issue. *137, 138*

Brown, J.A.C. (1961) *Freud and the Post-Freudians*, Harmondsworth, Penguin. *12*

Browne, J.A. and Howarth, E. (1977) 'A comprehensive factor analysis of personality questionnaire items: a test of twenty putative factor hypotheses, *Multivariate Behavioural Research*, 12, 399–427. *59*

Brozek, J. (1972) 'To test or not to test: trends in the Soviet view', *Journal of the History of the Behavioural Sciences*, 8, 243–8. *7*

Buros, O.K. (1974) *Tests in Print II*, New Jersey, Gryphon Press. *91*

Butler, F.J.J., Crinnion, J. and Martin, J. (1972) 'The Kuder Preference Record in adult vocational guidance', *Occupational Psychology*, 46, 99–104. *142*

Byrne, D., Barry, J. and Nelson, D. (1963) 'Relation of the revised Repression–Sensitization Scale to measures of self-description', *Psychological Reports*, 13, 323–34. *67*

Campbell, D. P. (1971) *Handbook for the Strong Vocational Interest Blank*, Stanford, California, Stanford University Press. *71*

Cattell, R. B. (1965) *The Scientific Analysis of Personality*, Harmondsworth, Penguin. *56, 57, 131*

Cattell, R. B. (1975) *New Morality from Science: Beyondism*, Oxford, Pergamon. *58*

Cattell, R.B., Eber, H.L. and Tatsuoka, M.M. (1970) *The 16PF Test*, Champaign, Illinois, Institute for Personality and Ability Testing. *58, 131*

Cattell, R.B. and Kline, P. (1977) *The Scientific Analysis of Personality and Motivation*, London, Academic Press. *57*

Christie, R. and Geis, F.L. (eds) (1970) *Studies in Machiavellianism*, New York, Academic Press. *66, 67*

Claridge, G.S. and Chappa, H.J. (1973) 'Psychoticism: a study of its biological basis in normal subjects', *British Journal of Social and Clinical Psychology*, 12, 175–87. *52*

Cook, M. (1982) 'Perceiving others: the psychology of interpersonal perception', Mackenzie Davey, D. and Harris, M. (eds) *Judging People*, London, McGraw-Hill. *84*

Cooper, R. and Payne, R. (1967) 'Extraversion and some aspects of work behaviour', *Personnel Psychology*, 20, 45–57. *134*

Coopersmith, S. (1967) *The Antecedents of Self Esteem*, San Francisco, W. H. Freeman. *65*

Coopersmith, S. (1968) 'Studies in self-esteem', *Scientific American*, 218, 96–106. *65*

Davies, D.R. and Shackleton, V.J. (1975) *Psychology and Work*, London, Methuen. *121*

Di Loreto, A.O. (1971) *Comparative Psychotherapy*, Chicago, Aldine-Atherton. *147*

Dipboye, R.L. and Wiley, J.W. (1977) 'Reactions of college recruiters to interviewee sex and self presentation style', *Journal of Vocational Behavior*, 10, 1–12. *100*

Dipboye, R.L. and Wiley, J.W. (1978) 'Reactions of male raters to interviewee self presentation style and sex; extensions of previous research', *Journal of Vocational Behavior*, 13, 192–203. *100*

Dulewicz, V. and Fletcher, C. (1982) 'The relationship between previous experience, intelligence and background characteristics of participants and their performance in an assessment centre', *Journal of Occupational Psychology*, 55, 197–207. *130*

Dymond, R.F. (1954) 'Interpersonal perception and marital happiness', *Canadian Journal of Psychology*, 8, 164–71. *84*

Elliott, C., Murray, D.J. and Pearson, L.S. (1983) *The British Ability Scales* (rev. edn), Windsor, Nelson-NFER. *93*

Endler, N.S. (1975) 'The care for person-situation interactions', *Canadian Psychological Review*, 16, 12–31. *48*

Epstein, S. (1979) 'The stability of behaviour: 1. On predicting most of the people most of the time', *Journal of Personality and Social Psychology*, 37, 1097–126. *47*

Ertl, J.P. (1971) 'Fourier analysis of evoked potentials and human intelligence', *Nature*, 230, 525–6. *29*

Ertl, J.P. and Schafer, E.W.P. (1969) 'Brain response correlates of psychometric intelligence, *Nature*, 223, 421–2. *29*

Eyferth, K. (1961) 'Leistungen verschiedener Gruppen von Besatzungs-kindern in Hamburg-Wechsler Intelligenztest für Kinder (HAWIK)', *Archiv für die desante Psychologie*, 113, 222–41, quoted in Willerman, L. (1979) *The Psychology of Individual and Group Differences*, San Francisco, W.H. Freeman, 448. *118*

Eysenck, H.J. (1947) *Dimensions of Personality*, London, Routledge & Kegan Paul. *49*

Eysenck, H.J. (1952a) *The Scientific Study of Personality*, London, Routledge & Kegan Paul. *48*

Eysenck, H.J. (1952b) 'The effects of psychotherapy: an evaluation', *Journal of Counselling Psychology*, 16, 319–24. *146*

Eysenck, H.J. (1963) 'Biological basis of personality', *Nature*, 199, 1031–4. *50*

Eysenck, H.J. (1965) 'Extraversion and the acquisition of eyeblink and GSR conditioned responses', *Psychological Bulletin*, 63, 258–70. *53*

Eysenck, H.J. (1966) *Check Your Own IQ*, Harmondsworth, Penguin. *107*

Eysenck, H.J. (1967) 'Personality patterns in various groups of business-men', *Occupational Psychology*, 41, 249–50. *132*

Eysenck, H.J. (1973) *The Inequality of Man*, London, Maurice Temple Smith. *113*

Eysenck, H.J. (1980) 'The bio-social nature of man and the unification of psychology', in Chapman, A.J. and Jones, D.M. (eds) *Models of Man*, London, British Psychological Society. *51*

Eysenck, H.J. and Eysenck, S.B.G. (1969) *Personality Structure and Measurement*, London, Routledge & Kegan Paul. *58*

Eysenck, H.J. and Eysenck, S.B.C. (1976) *Psychoticism as a Dimension of Personality*, London, Hodder & Stoughton. *50*

Eysenck, H.J. versus Kamin, L. (1981) *Intelligence: The Battle for the Mind*, London, Pan. *29, 30, 35, 36*

Eysenck, M.W. and Eysenck, H.J. (1980) 'Mischel and the concept of personality', *British Journal of Psychology*, 71, 71–83. *47*

Fairweather, H. (1976) 'Sex differences in cognition', *Cognition*, 4, 231–80. *109*

Fineman, S. (1977) 'The achievement motive construct and its measurement: where are we now?' *British Journal of Psychology*, 68, 1–22. *79*

Fletcher, C. (1981a) 'Candidates' beliefs and self-presentation strategies in selection interviews', *Personnel Review*, 10, 14–17. *100*

Fletcher, C. (1981b) *Facing the Interview*, London, Unwin Paperbacks. *100*

Fletcher, C. (1982) 'Assessment centres', in Mackenzie Davey, D. and Harris, M. (eds) *Judging People*, London, McGraw-Hill. *137*

Fletcher, C. and Dulewicz, V. (1984) 'An empirical study of a UK assessment centre', *Journal of Management Studies*, 21 (in press). *138*

Fonagy, P. (1981) 'Research on psychoanalytic concepts', in Fransella, F. (ed.) *Personality*, London, Methuen. *14*

Fonagy, P. (1984) *Personality Theories and Their Clinical Applications*, London, Methuen. *62*

Friedman, M. and Rosenman, R.H. (1974) *Type A Behaviour and Your Heart*, New York, Knopf. *68*

Gable, R.K. and Pruzek, R.M. (1971) 'Super's Work Values Inventory: two multivariate studies of inter-item relationships', *Journal of Experimental Education*, 40, 41–50. *76*

Geis, F. L. and Moon, T.H. (1981) 'Machiavellianism and deception', *Journal of Personality and Social Psychology*, 41, 766–75. *67*

Ghiselin, B. (ed.) (1952) *The Creative Process*, Berkeley, University of California Press. *41*

Ghiselli, E.E. (1963) 'Intelligence and managerial success', *Psychological Reports*, 12, 898. *130*

Ghiselli, E.E. (1966) *The Validity of Occupational Aptitude Tests*, New York, Wiley. *127, 128*

Ghiselli, E.E. (1973) 'The validity of aptitude tests in personnel selection', *Personnel Psychology*, 26, 461–77. *127*

Gill, R.W.T. (1982) 'A trainability concept for management potential and an empirical study of its relationship with intelligence for two managerial skills', *Journal of Occupational Psychology*, 55, 139–48. *130*

Gillie, O. (1976) *Who Do You Think You Are? Man or Superman: The Genetic Controversy*, London, Hart-Davis MacGibbon. *34*

Gomes-Schwartz, B., Hadley, S.W. and Strupp, H.H. (1978) 'Individual psychotherapy and behavior therapy', *Annual Review of Psychology*, 29, 435–72. *147*

Gould, S.J. (1981) *The Mismeasure of Man*, London: W.W. Norton. *23–24, 33*

Greer, S. and Morris, T. (1975) 'Psychological attributes of women who develop breast cancer: a controlled study', *Journal of Psychosomatic Research*, 19, 147–53. *149*

Hall, C.S. and Lindzey, G. (1957) *Theories of Personality*, New York, Wiley. *46*

Hearnshaw, L.S. (1979) *Cyril Burt: Psychologist*, Ithaca, New York, Cornell University Press. *33*

Heim, A. (1970) *The AH6 Group Tests of High Level Intelligence*, Windsor, NFER–Nelson. *93*

Hendrickson, D.E. and Hendrickson, A.E. (1980) 'The biological basis of individual differences in intelligence', *Personality and Individual Differences*, 1, 3–33. *29*

Heron, A. (1956) 'The effects of real-life motivation on questionnaire response', *Journal of Applied Psychology*, 40, 65–8. *133*

Herrman, L. and Hogben, L. (1932) 'The intellectual resemblance of twins', *Proceedings of the Royal Society of Edinburgh*, 53, 105–29. *31*

Hocevar, D. (1980) 'Intelligence, divergent thinking and creativity', *Intelligence*, 4, 25–40. *42*

Holland, J.L. (1973) *Making Vocational Choices: A Theory of Careers*, Englewood Cliffs, New Jersey, Prentice-Hall. *140*

Holmes, T.H. and Rahe, R.H. (1967) 'The Social Readjustment Rating Scale', *Journal of Psychosomatic Research*, 11, 213–18. *150*

Horner, M.S. (1972) 'Toward an understanding of achievement-related conflicts in women', *Journal of Social Issues*, 28, 157–76. *80*

Howarth, C.I. and Gillham, W.E.C. (1981) *The Structure of Psychology: An Introductory Text*, London, George Allen & Unwin. *41*

Huck, J.R. (1977) 'The research base', in Moses, J.L. and Byham, W.C. (eds) *Applying the Assessment Centre Method*, New York, Pergamon Press. *138*

Imboden, J.B., Canter, A. and Cluff, L.E. (1961) 'Convalescence from influenza: a study of the psychological and clinical determinants', *Archives of Internal Medicine*, 108, 393–9. *150*

Ingham, J.G., Robinson, J.O. and Rawnsley, K. (1961) 'Psychological field studies in defined populations, *Advancement of Science*, 18, 265–72. *53*

Ivey, A.E. (1963) 'Interests and work values', *Vocational Guidance Quarterly*, 11, 121–4. *77*

Jenkins, C.D. (1976) 'Recent evidence supporting psychologic and social risk factors for coronary disease'. *New England Journal of Medicine*, 294, 987–94 (part 1) 1033–8 (part 2). *68*

Jensen, A.R. (1981) 'The chronometry of intelligence', in Sternberg, R.J. (ed.) *Advances in Research on Intelligence*, 1, Hillsdale, New Jersey, Lawrence Erlbaum. *28*

Juel-Nielsen, N. (1965). 'Individual and environment: a psychiatric-psychological investigation of monozygotic twins reared apart', *Acta Psychiatrica et Neurologica Scandinavica*, Monograph Supplement, 183. *33*

Jung, C.G. (1928) 'Psychological types', in Semeonoff, B. (ed.) (1966) *Readings in Personality Assessment*, Harmondsworth, Penguin. *15*

Kamin, L. (1977) *The Science and Politics of IQ*, Harmondsworth, Penguin. *30, 35*

Katzell, R.A. (1964) 'Personal values, job satisfaction and job behaviour', in Berow, H. (ed.) *Man in a World at Work*, New York, Houghton-Mifflin. *74*

Kleemeier, R.W. (1962) 'Intellectual change in the senium', *Proceedings of the American Statistical Association*, 290–5. *122*

Kline, P. (1976) *Psychological Testing: The Measurement of Intelligence, Ability and Personality*, London, Malaby Press. *72, 73*

Kline, P. (1981a) *Fact and Fantasy in Freudian Theory*, 2nd edn, London, Methuen. *14*

Kline, P. (1981b) 'Recent research into the factor analysis of personality', in Fransella, F. (ed.) *Personality*, London, Methuen. *59*

Kline, P. (1983) *Personality: Measurement and Theory*, London, Hutchinson. *47*

Kluckhohn, C., Murray, H.A. and Schneider, D.M. (eds) (1953) *Personality in Nature, Society and Culture*, New York, Knopf. *5*

Korman, A.K. (1976) 'Hypothesis of work behavior revisited and an extension', *Academy of Management Review*, 1, 50–63. *65*

Kraut, A.I. (1969) 'Intellectual ability and promotional success among high level managers, *Personnel Psychology*, 22, 281–90. *130*

Kraut, R.E. and Paice, J.D. (1976) 'Machiavellianism in parents and their children', *Journal of Personality and Social Psychology*, 33, 782–6. *66*

Kyriacou, C. and Sutcliffe, J. (1979) 'A note on teacher stress and locus of control', *Journal of Occupational Psychology*, 52, 227–8. *135*

Latané, B. and Darley, J.M. (1970) *The Unresponsive Bystander: Why Doesn't He Help?* New York, Appleton Century Crofts. *47*

Lefcourt, H.M. (1982) *Locus of Control*, 2nd edn, Hillsdale, New Jersey, Lawrence Erlbaum. *66*

Levenson, H. (1973) 'Reliability and validity of the I, P and C scales: a multidimensional view of locus of control', *Proceedings of the 81st Annual Convention of the American Psychological Association*, cited in Green, R.G. (1976) *Personality*, St Louis, Mosby. *147*

Lykken, D. (1981) *A Tremor in the Blood*, New York, McGraw-Hill. *103*

Mabe, P.A. and West, S.G. (1982) 'Validity of self-evaluation of ability: a review and meta-analysis', *Journal of Applied Psychology*, 67, 280–96. *100*

McClelland, D.C. (1951) *Personality*, New York, William Sloan. *78*

McClelland, D.C. and Winter, D.C. (1969) *Motivating Economic Achievement*, New York, Free Press. *135*

Maccoby, E.E. and Jacklin, C.N. (1975) *The Psychology of Sex Differences*, London, Oxford University Press. *105*

Mackenzie Davey, D. and Harris, M. (eds) (1982) *Judging People*, London, McGraw-Hill. *104*

Matarazzo, J.D. (1972) *Wechsler's Measurement and Appraisal of Adult Intelligence*, 5th edn, Baltimore, Maryland, Williams & Wilkins. *123*

Meehl, P.E. (1954) *Clinical vs. Statistical Prediction*, Minneapolis, University of Minnesota Press. *138*

Milgram, S. (1974) *Obedience to Authority*, London, Tavistock. *111*

Minter, R.E. and Kimball, C.P. (1980) 'Life events, personality traits and illness', in Kutash, I.L. and Schlesinger, C.B. (eds) *Handbook on Stress and Anxiety*, San Francisco, Josey-Bass. *150*

Mischel, W. (1968) *Personality and Assessment*, New York, Wiley. *47*

Mischel, W. (1977) 'The interaction of person and situation', in Magnussen, D. and Endler, N.S. (eds) *Personality at the Crossroads: Current Issues in Interactional Psychology*, Hillsdale, New Jersey, Lawrence Erlbaum. *48*

Mogul, K.M. (1982) 'Overview: the sex of the therapist', *American Journal of Psychiatry*, 139, 1–11. *147*

Myers, I.B. (1980) *Introduction to Type*, 3rd edn, Palo Alto, California, Consulting Psychologists Press. *16*

Neuhas, E.C. (1958) 'A personality study of asthmatic and cardiac children', *Psychosomatic Medicine*, 20, 181–6. *149*

Newman, H.H., Freeman, F.N. and Holzinger, K.J. (1937) *Twins: A Study of Heredity and Environment*, Chicago, University of Chicago Press. *33*

Nicholson, J. (1979) *A Question of Sex: The Differences Between Men and Women*, London, Fontana. *110, 111*

Open University (1974) *Psychometrics*, Units 4–6 of course DS261, 'An Introduction to Psychology', Milton Keynes, Bucks, Open University Press. *19*

Pandey, J. and Tewary, N.B. (1979) 'Locus of control and achievement values of entrepreneurs, *Journal of Occupational Psychology*, 52, 107–12. *134*

Peck, D. and Whitlow, D. (1975) *Approaches to Personality Theory*, London, Methuen. *65*

Pettit, I.B., Pettit, T.F. and Welkowitz J. (1974) 'Relationship between values, social class and duration of psychotherapy', *Journal of Consulting and Clinical Psychology*, 42, 482–90. *147*

Piaget, J. (1954) *The Construction of Reality in the Child*, New York, Basic Books. *27*

Poppleton, S.E. (1975) 'Biographical and personality characteristics associated with the success in life assurance salesmen', M. Phil. thesis, Birkbeck College, University of London. *95*

Pryor, R.G.L. (1978) *The Second Report on the Construction of the Work Aspect Scale*, New South Wales, Australia, Department of Industrial Relations Technology, Central Planning and Research Unit. *75*

Pryor, R.G.L. (1980) *Research Report: Values, Needs, Work Ethics and Orientations to Work: Towards a Conceptual and Empirical Integration*, New South Wales, Australia, Department of Industrial Relations Technology, Central Planning and Research Unit. *74*

Pryor, R.G.L. (1981) *Manual for the Work Aspect Preference Scale*, New

South Wales, Australia, Department of Industrial Relations Technology, Central Planning and Research Unit. *76*

Rachman, S.J. and Phillips, C. (1978) *Psychology and Medicine*, Harmondsworth, Penguin. *150*

Rahe, R.H., Mahan J.L. and Arthur, R.J. (1970) 'Prediction of near-future health change from subjects preceding life changes', *Journal of Psychosomatic Research*, 14, 401–6. *150*

Rawles, R.E. (1981) Review of H.J. Eysenck versus L. Kamin, *Intelligence: the Battle for the Mind*, in, London, Pan, *The Times Higher Education Supplement*, 24 April 1981. *31*

Revelle, W., Humphreys, M.S., Simon, L. and Gilliland, K. (1980) 'The interactive effect of personality, time of day and caffeine: a test of the arousal model', *Journal of Experimental Psychology*, 109, 1–29. *53*

Robertson, I.T. and Kandola, R.S. (1982) 'Work sample tests: validity, adverse impact and applicant reaction', *Journal of Occupational Psychology*, 55, 171–84. *102*

Rogers, C.R. and Dymond, R.F. (1954) *Psychotherapy and Personality Change*, Chicago, University of Chicago Press. *101*

Rokeach, M. (1973) *The Nature of Human Values*, New York, Free Press. *74, 76*

Rosen, A. (1966) 'Stability of new MMPI scales and statistical procedures for evaluating changes and differences in psychiatric patients', *Journal of Consulting Psychology*, 30, 142–5. *148*

Rosenthal, R. and Jacobson, L. (1968) *Pygmalion in the Classroom: Teacher Expectation and Pupils' Intellectual Development*, New York, Holt, Rinehart & Winston. *26*

Ross, L. (1977) 'The intuitive psychologist and his shortcomings: distortions in the attribution process, *Advances in Experimental Social Psychology*, 10, 174–220. *47*

Ross, M.W., Kalucy, R.S. and Morton, J.E. (1983) 'Locus of control in obesity: predictors of success in a jaw-wiring programme', *British Journal of Medical Psychology*, 56, 49–56. *146*

Rotter, J.B. (1954) *Social Learning in Clinical Psychology*, Englewood Cliffs, New Jersey, Prentice-Hall. *66*

Rotter, J.B. (1966) 'Generalized expectancies for internal versus external control of reinforcement', *Psychological Monographs*, 80 (1) (whole issue no. 609). *66*

Rust, J. (1975) 'Cortical evoked potential, personality and intelligence', *Journal of Comparative and Physiological Psychology*, 89, 1220–6. *29*

Sauls, J.M. and Larson, R.C. (1975) *Exploring Rational Assessment Data using Singular Value Decomposition*, Denver, Colorado, Educational Commission of the United States, April 1975. *109*

Savage, R.D. and Stewart, R.R. (1972) 'Personality and the success of card-punch operators in timing', *British Journal of Psychology*, 63, 445–50. *134*

Saville, P. and Blinkhorn, S. (1976) *Undergraduate Personality by Factored Scales*, Windsor, National Foundation for Educational Research. *59*

Scarpetti, W.L. (1973) 'The repression-sensitization dimension in relation to impending painful stimulation', *Journal of Consulting and Clinical Psychology*, 40, 377–82. *67*

Scarr, S. and Weinberg, R.A. (1976) IQ test performance of black children adopted by white families. *American Psychologist*, 31, 726–39. *118*

Schiff, M. Duyme, M., Dumaret, A., Stewart, J., Tomkiewicz, S. and Feingold, J. (1978) Intellectual status of working-class children adopted early into upper middle-class families', *Science*, 200, 1503–4. *36*

Schmidt, F.L. and Hunter, J.E. (1981) 'Employment testing: old theories and new research findings', *American Psychologist*, 36, 1128–37. *129*

Schwab, D.P. *American Psychologist*, 31, 726–39. *118*

Schwab, D.P. and Packard, G.L. (1973) 'Response distortion on the Gordon Personal Inventory and the Gordon Personal Profile in a selection context – some implications for predicting employee turnover', *Journal of Applied Psychology*, 58, 372–4. *133*

Serbin, L.A., O'Leary, K.D., Kent, R.N. and Tonick, I.J.A. (1973) 'A comparison of teacher response to the pre-academic and problem behaviour of boys and girls', *Child Development*, 44, 796–804. *112*

Shackleton, V.J. (1980) 'The accountancy stereotype: myth or reality?' *Accountancy*, 91, 122–3. *70*

Shackleton, V.J. and Engel, J.D. (1982) 'Report on work values and their relationship to occupational choice', unpublished report, University of Aston, Birmingham. *74*

Shackleton, V.J. and Fletcher, C. (1973) 'Psychiatric patients' motivation in an assessment situation: implications arising from recent work', *Bulletin of the British Psychological Society*, 26, 17–23. *96*

Shackleton, V.J. and Spurgeon, P.C. (1982) 'The relative importance of potential outcomes of occupational guidance: an assessment by occupational guidance officers', *Journal of Occupational Psychology*, 55, 191–5. *141*

Sheehan, T. (1977) 'Breast cancer and personality', unpublished dissertation, California School of Professional Psychology, San Diego. *149*

Shields, J. (1962) *Monozygotic Twins*, London, Oxford University Press. *33, 34*

Shrauger, J.S. and Osberg, T.M. (1981) 'The relative accuracy of self-predictions and judgements by others in psychological assessment', *Psychological Bulletin*, 90, 322–51. *100, 142*

Shuey, A.M. (1966) *The Testing of Negro Intelligence*, 2nd edn, New York, Social Science Press. *117*

Singleton, C.H. (1978) 'Sex differences', in Foss, B.M. (ed.) *Psychology Survey*, 1, London, Allen & Unwin. *113*

Smith, M.L. and Glass, C.V. (1977) 'Meta-analysis of psychotherapy outcome studies, *American Psychologist*, 32, 752–60. *147*

Spitzer, R.L. and Fleiss, J.L. (1974) 'A re-analysis of the reliability of psychiatric diagnosis', *British Journal of Psychiatry*, 125, 341–7. *143*

Sternbach, R.A., Wolf, S.R., Murphy, R.W. and Akeson, W.H. (1973) 'Traits of pain patients: the low-back "loser"', *Psychosomatics*, 14, 226–9. *149*

Sterns, L., Alexander, R.A., Barrett, G. V. and Dambrot, F.H. (1983) 'The relationship of extraversion and neuroticism with job preferences and job satisfaction for clerical employees', *Journal of Occupational Psychology*, 56, 145–54. *134*

Strong, E.K. (1951) 'Permanence of interest scores over 22 years', *Journal of Applied Psychology*, 35, 89–91. *124*

Super, D.E. (1962) 'The structure of work values in relation to status, achievement, interests and adjustment', *Journal of Applied Psychology*, 46, 231–9. *77*

Super, D.E. (1973) 'The work values inventory', in Zytowski, D.G. (ed.) *Contemporary Approaches and Interest Measurement*, Minneapolis, University of Minnesota Press. *75*

Swenson, W.M., Pearson, J.S. and Osborne, D. (1973) *An MMPI Source Book: Basic Item, Scale and Pattern Data on 50,000 Medical Patients*, Minneapolis, University of Minnesota Press. *123*

Thelen, M.H. (1969) 'Repression-sensitization: its relation to adjustment and seeking psychotherapy among college students', *Journal of Consulting and Clinical Psychology*, 33, 161–5. *67*

Thorndike, R.M., Weiss, D.J. and Dawis, R.V. (1968) 'Canonical correlations of vocational needs', *Journal of Counselling Psychology*, 15, 101–6. *77*

Thornton, G.C. (1978) 'Differential effects of career planning on internals and externals', *Personnel Psychology*, 31, 471–6. *134*

Turner, J. (1984) *Cognitive Development and Education*, London, Methuen. *27*

Tyler, L.E. (1965) *The Psychology of Human Differences*, 3rd edn, New York, Appleton-Century-Crofts. *105*

Vagg, P.R. and Hammond, S.B. (1976) 'The number and kind of invariant personality Q factors: a partial replication of Eysenck and Eysenck', *British Journal of Social and Clinical Psychology*, 15, 121–30. *58*

Vernon, P.E. (1953) *Personality Tests and Assessments*, London, Methuen. *137*

Vernon, P.E. (1964) *Personality Assessment: A Critical Survey*, London, Methuen. *63*

Vernon, P.E. (ed.) (1973) *Creativity*, Harmondsworth, Penguin. *40, 103*

Vernon, P.E. (1979) *Intelligence: Heredity and Environment*, San Francisco, W.H. Freeman. *27, 33, 39*

Watts, A.G. and Kidd, J.M. (1978) 'Evaluating the effectiveness of careers guidance: a review of the British research', *Journal of Occupational Psychology*, 51, 235–48. *142*

Weiner, B. (1980) *Human Motivation*, New York, Holt, Rinehart & Winston.

Welsh, F. (1982) 'Judging people: the early background', in Mackenzie Davey, D. and Harris, M. (eds) *Judging People*, London, McGraw-Hill. *12*

Willerman, L. (1979) *The Psychology of Individual and Group Differences*, San Francisco, W.H. Freeman. *116, 117*

Willerman, L., Naylor, A.F. and Myrianthopoulos, N.C. (1974) 'Intelligence development of children from interracial matings: performance in infancy and at four years', *Behavior Genetics*, 4, 83–90. *118*

Williams, J.D., Dudley, H.K. and Oberall, J.E. (1972) 'Validity of the 16PF and the MMPI in a mental hospital setting', *Journal of Abnormal Psychology*, 80, 261–70. *58*

Wilson, G.D., Tunstall, D.A. and Eysenck, H.J. (1972) 'Measurements of motivation in predicting industrial performance', *Developmental Psychology*, 46, 15–24. *134*

Winter, D.G. (1973) *The Power Motive*, New York, Free Press. *81*

Winterbottom, M.R. (1958) 'The relation of need for achievement to learning experiences in independence and mastery', in Atkinson, J.W. (ed.) *Motives in Fantasy, Action and Society*, Princeton, New Jersey, Van Nostrand. *80*

Wittig, M.A. and Petersen, A.C. (1978) *Sex Differences in Cognitive Functioning: Developmental Issues*, New York, Academic Press. *106*

Wollowick, H.B. and McNamara, W.J. (1969) 'Relationship of the components of an assessment centre to management success', *Journal of Applied Psychology*, 53, 348–52. *138*

Woodruff, D.S. and Birren, J.E. (1972) Age changes and cohort differences in personality, *Developmental Psychology*, 6, 252–9. *124*

Wright, D.S., Taylor, A., Davies, D.R., Sluckin, W., Lee, S.G.M. and Reason, J.T. (1970) *Introducing Psychology*, Harmondsworth, Penguin. *46*

Zytowski, D.G. (1970) 'The concept of work values', *Vocational Guidance Quarterly*, 18, 176–86. *77*

Subject index

The references section of this book serves as a name index. Names are included in this index only where there is no corresponding literature citation; in most cases these are the names of historical personages.